OBAMA
meets
AHMADINEJAD

"Amil Imani reveals a wickedly cutting satirist's eye as he sketches out an acidly funny meeting between Barack Obama—imagined as a sharp-tongued but supine secret Sunni Muslim—and Mahmoud Ahmadinejad, who is determined to remove the Great Satan as an obstacle in the way of the advance of Shi'ite Muslim world domination. As they spar verbally, Ahmadinejad runs circles around the hapless Obama, and in the course of the conversations reveals a great deal about Islamic supremacism, Iran, the Sunni/Shi'ite divide, and more. It's a dystopian fantasy, but with Obama appearing determined to appease the Islamic world at all costs, it's strikingly illuminating of the present-day predicament of America and the West."

> —Robert Spencer, author of the New York Times bestsellers *The Politically Incorrect Guide to Islam (and the Crusades)* and *The Truth About Muhammad*

"Although a great work of fiction which at times resembles reality, this book is a fantastic, powerful and hilarious creative writing by Amil Imani. I'll be recommending it to all my colleagues."

> —Dr. Wafa Sultan, author of *A God Who Hates: The Courageous Woman Who Inflamed the Muslim World Speaks Out Against the Evils of Islam*

"In *Obama Meets Ahmadinejad*, 'democracy is so flawed that it can be imploded from within.' The president of Iran wants to make sure that the march of Islam won't be stopped. He browbeats and bullies the naive and arrogant U.S. president in a series of secret meetings that Amil Imani vividly imagines—or transcribes—in this funny, insightful and illuminating book. Satire or accurate reportage? In today's morally inverted world, what's the difference?"

"Charlie Chaplin was aware of the great power of ridicule. A strong opponent of racism, in 1937 Chaplin decided to make a film on the dangers of fascism. Attempts were made to stop the film being made, 'but I was determined to go ahead, for Hitler must be laughed at,' wrote Chaplin in his Autobiography.

"In this parody, Amil Imani ridicules two dangerous zanies of our time, who also must be laughed at, who both have deceitfully usurped their presidency, and together are bringing the world to the brink of Armageddon.

"Imani is a powerful writer. Have your dictionary handy and enjoy this exquisite literature."

OBAMA
meets
AHMADINEJAD

Amil Imani

Disclaimer

The following is a work of fiction, parody and satire.
Any resemblance to actual people and places is strictly
coincidental. The opinions here are not necessarily
those of the author or his supporters.

Free American Press
www.AmilImani.com

Library of Congress Cataloguing in Publication Data
Imani, Amil
 Obama Meets Ahmadinejad
 1. Political satire—Fiction 2. Politics—Parody
ISBN-13: 9781926800028

Printed in USA

Publisher: Felibri.com

Felibri publications are distributed by Ingram Book
Group

Dedication

This book is dedicated to the past, to the present and to the future defenders of freedom anywhere in the world: to those exemplary women and men who resisted and continue to resist religious and secular tyranny, who have paid and are willing to pay the ultimate price. A young woman, Neda Agha Sultan, and a young man, Sohrab, whose lives were extinguished by the brutal Islamic Regime of Iran, I name here as representative of all champions of liberty.

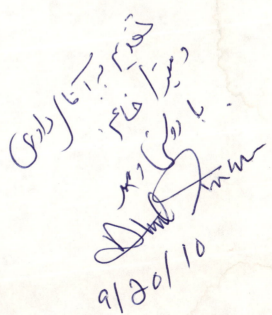

Table of Contents

Glossary

adhan—the Muslim call to prayer, practiced five times a day

ana—the personal pronoun "I"

Atefeh Rajabi Sahaaleh—a 16-year-old Iranian girl who was executed after she had been raped by a judge

ayah—a verse from the Quran/Koran

ayatollah—a title for a high-ranking Islamic scholar in the Twelver Shi'a sect

Baha'i—an independent monotheistic religion that embraces all revealed faiths

Basij—the volunteer militia founded by Ayatollah Ruhollah Khomeini

Dar al-Harb—the "house of war," the lands of the *kuffar* or infidels

Dar al-Islam—the "house of Islam," the lands supposedly belonging to Muslims

dhimmi—a non-Muslim who lives under Muslim domination and sharia law

Haya ala al jihad—part of the *adhan* or Muslim call to prayer, meaning, "Hasten ye to jihad"

Houri—a young virgin girl promised to faithful Muslim men in the Islamic Paradise

hugheh—a "pipe"

imam—a common Muslim spiritual leader

Jamkaran well—a "sacred site" in Iran in which the Twelfth Imam or Mahdi is said to be waiting, to return to earth after more than 1,000 years

jihad—Islamic "struggle" against "evil," both within and outside as concerns non-belief and infidels jinn—a supernatural being living in a parallel world; genie

Ka'aba—the cube-shaped building at the sacred site of Mecca that houses the holy meteorite

kafir, kuffar—"apostate(s)," "unbeliever(s)"

kaka siah—a derogatory term for a black person

kalemaate-al-Ghesaar—a collection of sayings attributed to Imam Ali

kitman—the act of hiding Islamic belief in order to advance jihad

Mahdi—the prophesied Islamic messiah and world-conqueror expected by many Muslims, both Sunni and Shi'a

manghal va vaafoor—a charcoal burner and pipe

manzel—"house," a degrading Shi'ite reference to one's wife

mullah—a Muslim "vicar" or clergyman

mutah—a temporary "marriage" contract or sexual contract that allows Muslim men to have sex with women who are not their "real" wives

nahno—the personal pronoun "we"

najis—"unclean," often used to refer to dogs and other creatures to be avoided by devout Muslims

Qom—the Iranian holy city where the Mahdi has resided in a well for over 1,000 years, according to Shi'a Islam

Rasul Allah—Messenger of Allah, Muhammad, Mohammed

Sahib al-Zaman, Imam Zaman Mahdi—Master of Time; Lord of the Age; the Twelfth Imam; or Mahdi, the coming Muslim Messiah

GLOSSARY iii

Sayed Al Shohada—Imam Hussein, grandson of Muhammad and founder of Shi'a Islam

sigheh—a temporary wife whom Muslim men may marry for any length of time, from a few hours or for as long as they wish

sharia—Islamic law

shaeron majnoon—the "Crazed Poet, a derogatory name for Muhammad

S*haytan al-raheem*—"the sinister Satan" or "Satan the sinister"

taqiyya—in Shi'ite Islam, "concealment," "deception," "dissimulation" or "lying" to infidels to further the cause of the faith

Ummah—the Islamic community of believers globally

zakat, zakah—the payment to Muslim charities only that comes from Islamic or sharia banking/finance

Preface

By now everyone knows about Obama's surprise trip to Afghanistan a while back. That's old news. What people don't know about is the side trip Obama made to Iran to meet with none other than the charming president of the Islamic Republic himself, the little fellow with a big ambition of turning the world into one huge fireball with Israel at its epicenter. This little fellow, Ahmadinejad, longs to do things that would make the heinous deeds of Hitler seem like the works of a model three-badger Boy Scout by comparison.

As usual, the lapdog liberal press, per its command from the powers-that-be, did not bark a word about these meetings. But, I am old-fashioned. I don't kowtow to any power. Nor do I aspire to be like the paragon of honest journalism, FOXNews. You've heard FOXNews blare, *ad infinitum*, "We report, you decide." What they don't tell you is that *they* make the important decisions about what is worthy of reporting.

As for me, I am a lone ranger, a maverick, really. I believe in the First Amendment and the freedom of the press. To me, freedom means just that, freedom. Not only do I select what I report, I also pass judgment freely. Give me credit—I am at least honest about my dishonesty, and that's a whole lot better than the dishonest people who go about being dishonest and pretending to be honest.

I confess right off the bat that I fully realize that eavesdropping is reprehensible, if not outright criminal. Yet, knowing this fact did not stop me from so doing, because I felt that, in dealing with Islamists like Ahmadinejad, it is in the spirit of fair play to level the playing field. As an ex-Muslim, I know that your "average" Muslim may be taught that the goal justifies the means: That is, if the goal is important, you say and do whatever it takes to achieve it. So I abided by the Islamic ethos and recorded the proceedings without their knowledge. Aren't we advised, when in Rome do as the Romans do? I lived right in the heart of a Muslim land, and I can attest that the Islamic rule is, "Do unto others what you never want others to do to you."

You might rightfully wonder how I, a one-man seat-of-the-pants operation sorely lacking funds, could have found out about the meetings, much less have managed to videotape every minute of them. And I, in turn, rightfully refuse to divulge the means of doing so, since it would be like shooting myself in the foot or even higher, right? Yet manage it, I did. I found out about the event well in advance, and bugged the location with hidden cameras and recording devices to capture everything that took place in the incredible multi-session *tête-à-tête*.

To help you appreciate better what transpired between the two self-adulating leaders, I have taken great pains to report to you their exact conversations to the limits of my ability. Keep in mind that English is not my native tongue, and if I screw up reporting, it is not a major journalistic violation, particularly since I am reporting about two of the worst screwballs the world has ever seen. Also, I was compelled to sanitize their language, which was at times juvenile, disgusting, profane and much more. I have also taken the liberty of reporting some of the exchanges in their original languages, providing translations, and in some cases I have put their statements in my own words, not to distort anything but to make them more comprehensible to you, the reader.

Beside the fact that this remarkable gathering took place, other aspects of the historical event struck me. For one, the *tête-à-tête* followed no prepared agenda. It was more like an exercise in free association, to say whatever you like at any point. Stick to a subject or raise a completely unrelated issue. The two repeated themselves, contradicted themselves and frequently acted like what psychologists call "manic-depressives." As for me, the innocent observer, the whole thing was one long exercise in suffering. I have never been able to suffer fools gladly, as advised—one of my many failings.

The interpersonal dynamics were most interesting. At times, deathly hostility peppered the speech of the little fellow, way out of proportion to his puny size. Obama, by contrast, tried but did not completely succeed in maintaining his composure, displaying an idiotic grin in retaliation, while aiming to ridicule Ahmadinejad—not exactly a task requiring the mind of a rocket scientist to do so, since the creep *personifies* ridicule, in addition to many other reprehensible traits. Yet, at other times, the two behaved toward one another with affection, camaraderie and admiration. I have tried to make sense of this mishmash, but I couldn't quite figure it all out. Perhaps you, the reader, can.

Without further ado, here is what happened. (My comments are in italics...)

Act One

"All the world's a stage, and all the men and women merely players..."

William Shakespeare, *As You Like It*

*A*lsalam-o-alayk ya akhi—*"peace be upon you, my brother"—intones Obama, with the trademark smirk he peddles as a smile, as Ahmadinejad enters the room. The little tyrant grins and nods his head in return, indicating his approval of hearing the phony American's Islamic greeting in Arabic. Surprisingly, Ahmadinejad gives Obama the "Texas Longhorns" two-fingered salute—I'd heard about it but was shocked to see what is supposed to be a "sign of Satan" or Masonic signal that has been made by dozens of power elite around the world. I wondered what it all could mean, but I guessed it indicated their brotherhood beyond all other boundaries, such as race, religion or nationality.*

Next, the puny fascist runs his claws over his scraggy whiskers, produces his own equally stomach-turning smirk, clears his throat and returns the greeting also in Arabic: Va alayk alsalam ya akhi al aziz—"and peace be upon you, my dear brother"—adding, "How you doing, old buddy?" in English.

As I watched the tape, I didn't think it at all surprising that both men spoke Arabic. Ahmadinejad speaking English, however, threw me for a loop and took me a minute or two to recover. Obama for his part also surprised me some. Given his sycophantic personality—

kissing up to important people—he did not bow deeply to the creep.

Then the usual full-body hug and three pecks on each cheek followed. The "American" fraud was visibly nervous. He seemed to be afraid that the zany zealot might shove a nasty knife into him for his crime of being an apostate.

According to Islamic or sharia law, being sired by a Muslim makes someone a Muslim, and the Fraud's father was a Sunni Muslim. Leaving Islam makes him an apostate and earns him an automatic death sentence. For devoted true Muslims, killing an apostate punches their tickets to Allah's lush sensual Paradise. So it was understandable that the guy was a bit jittery.

THE FASCIST

> Ah, it is good to see you visiting our part of the world, as the disputed election and following Green Movement kept us apart for a while. My enemies claim I stole 25 million votes from Mousavi in that election, can you believe?! But I have crushed my opposition once again! A million thanks to you, Hussein—our great saint's namesake—for not "meddling" with our family business. It was truly genius using the word "meddle," as if it was just some little squabble between lovers. Although you may rightly think me your intellectual superior, I have learned from even your own political campaign: I borrowed your slogan, "YES, WE CAN"—and it worked!

With that, the repulsive despot let the first of many revolting howls the Fraud and I would have to endure throughout their meetings.

THE FASCIST

> Anyway, we are very pleased to have you in front of us, where we want you. We are doubly pleased with your Arabic speech. It sounds

perfect. We mean, it *is* perfect for our plan. Perfect. Again, it is very good indeed to meet you, because we have much to discuss—especially about your apostasy. As you know, it is intolerable to us, so we are offering you a way out, although we should just kill you on the spot.

Also, we cannot refrain ourself from rushing to the truth—it troubles us to no end to see the murdering American troops maiming and killing our co-religionists next door to us here in Afghanistan. Some say that you also have *us* in your crosshairs. In truth, I hope that it is all rumors—our brotherhood does not find any of it amusing.

I noticed that the wretch began to switch back and forth from using the pronoun "I" to the "royal we," which to me signaled a split-personality problem. This behavior would continue throughout the session, making it difficult at times to figure out if he was referring to himself alone or to himself and the rest of his gang of thugs.

THE FRAUD

Well, during my presidential campaign in 2007, I did say that I would meet with you, so here I am. After your invitation following your nuclear fuel-swap deal with Turkey, I decided it was time.

But I see we're just jumping right in—they told me you were rude and rough, but I thought our amicable and brotherly start might slow down your onslaught of complaints. How many Iranians marched in the streets in protest of your rigged election? Did you say FIVE MILLION? Five million people calling for your head? Are you not worried?

In any case, don't blame *me* for American troops being in Afghanistan. That was done by my predecessor, and I am doing my level best to bring the criminal campaign he launched to an end as quickly as I possibly can, but I've been put under pressure to put in more troops instead. Keep in mind that an American President can't run things by fiat, as is the case in your country. I mean, the Iranian Supreme Leader, Ayatollah Ali Khamenei, has that power. He can do anything he wants. All he has to do is say the word, and it is done. You also, as President of the Islamic Republic, have incredible authority to do just about everything you want as long as you clear it with the Leader. As for me, I have to go through endless hoops before I can even pick my own nose...

THE FASCIST

You are picking your nose right this minute, and I did not see you go through even a single hoop.

Immediately showing his true vulgar colors, the little tyrant unleashed another round of booming, convulsing, disgusting laughter, while the Fraud quickly extracted his finger, stretched his smirk a bit wider and waited for the hyena to de-convulse. If nothing else, these two clowns were good for a hearty laugh.

THE FRAUD

I'm glad I made you laugh, I guess. I wouldn't want to piss you off! How many innocent people did you personally kill when you were a Revolutionary Guard, anyway? Hundreds? Thousands?

THE FASCIST

What impudence! Have you forgotten you are a filthy apostate, worthy of death? We could have you killed right now—as you point out, we could do it ourself. Instead, I suggest you comply with what I am going to propose to you. Have the American boys pack and leave Afghanistan, and while you are at it, pull the rest of your killers out of Iraq. We say "your," as if you are really an American! But, we know better, do we not?

We digress. If you pull out the American troops, the leftists and peaceniks will love you for it, and even the hawks would have to keep their damned mouths shut, since you would be saving the nation a fortune. You contract the job to us in the region, just the way the U.S. dealt with the accursed Shah. He was the American errand-boy policeman and wielded a big stick. Nobody dared to make trouble while he walked his beat, so to speak. Now, we are not going to be like him, the American puppet that he was. We want things in return. Reasonable stuff, believe me. You will love the offers we make you. Are you interested?

THE FRAUD

Sure, sure—that's why I am here, isn't it? Speaking of the Shah of Iran, when American President Jimmy Carter took office in 1977, the Shah was a staunch ally of the United States, a mainstay in our standoff with the Soviet Union, thwarting the dream held since the time of the czars of pushing south toward the warm waters of the Persian Gulf. I suppose the Shah was becoming too nationalistic for his own good, so, the Americans just tossed him out. You wouldn't be here if we had not done that. Give us Americans more credit—we created the green belt of Islam, got rid of the Shah, and for that you should be thankful. So, we know how to play ball.

THE FASCIST

> Ha! "*Us* Americans?" Do not take any personal credit, friend, as you were just a kid doing cocaine in high school at the time. In any case, fine, let us proceed. I will give you the broad outline. If you play, then we will work out the details. Okay?

THE FRAUD

> Go ahead and tell me.

THE FASCIST

> First about Iraq, and then I will get to the matter of Afghanistan. By now, you know all about our great influence in Iraq. Our plan is that we call off our dogs there. We let the Shi'a, the Sunni, the Kurd, the Turkeman and the lot, work things out so that they all get a fair share of the action. It is all about oil money. They all want it, and we will see to it that all get a fair share of it. We will twist arms—we are very good at it. You ought to know that too by now. We will do whatever it takes to have all the dogs get their piece of the oil carcass. And we will see to it that oil keeps flowing non-stop, just the way the American oil-junkies like it.

> Also, in no way do we want to turn Iraq into another Shi'a Islamic Republic like ours. It will not work there, and we know it. We will let them have their gift called democracy that you have given them and see how it plays out. Are you with me?

THE FRAUD

> Using *taqiyya*—lying—again, are you? Of course I'm with you. Who the hell do you think I am with, the devil? You may think I'm an apostate, but when have I ever shown myself to be hostile to Islam and Allah?

THE FASCIST

> You cover your buttocks now, but even so your father's Sunni sect is a heresy—so you remain an apostate. Do not think you can pull a fast one on me! Now, about our deal—

THE FRAUD

> I know all about the "fair" deals you offer: You take 100 percent, and I get the rest. You win, I lose. A real fair deal.

> It reminds me of the time my grandmother, bless her soul, came with me to help me buy my first car. The salesman, a shifty, fast-talking little creep, kept saying that he liked me and that he was going to give me not just a fair deal but "the best deal of my young life." My trusting grandma—bless her soul, such a trusting soul she was....

> My grannie went for the crook's sales pitch and bought the car for me, paying almost double what it was worth. The damned jalopy threw a rod only two days later when I took it to school to show off my set of wheels. Not even the junkyard would give us a dime for it. My grandma, bless her soul, had to pay to have it towed away before the police cited us for illegally keeping a wreck parked in the street—

THE FASCIST

> Before you go on, tell us, was "Bless Her Soul" her name? Unusual, never heard anyone by such name—perhaps we should follow her, since we like to worship people with the same sort of megalomaniacal titles....

Then the evil troll ended his interruption with a long laugh.

THE FRAUD

Let me finish the story. I swear you could be that salesman incarnate, or at least his double, just as ugly, shifty and fast-talking, offering people deals of their life out of the cruelness of your heart. I have a request: I am asking you, please don't even use that word "truth." Hearing it out of your foul mouth gives me the willies. Speaking of which, you remind me of "Slick Willy," also known as William Jefferson Clinton. You must certainly remember how he demanded people define what truth was? Well, *he* didn't know what truth was, never had any use for it, and got to the top without it.

THE FASCIST

Yes, yes, we do remember that reprehensible jackass who—much to the chagrin of the Americans—was too busy with that young Jewess Mossad agent Monica Lewinsky to take care of Osama bin Laden, while the renegade Sheik was supposed to be roaming freely about in Africa exploding buildings and frying people. "Slick" left the task to that big-mouth cowboy George W. Bush, who bragged foolishly that he would smoke bin Laden out of his cave in Afghanistan, first bathing him on a water-board before executing him. Empty bravado, I say, especially since we know where bin Laden really was hiding out—

At this point, the Fraud jumped up excitedly, practically throwing himself at the Fascist's feet. I was stunned to see this sycophantic behavior since thus far he had managed to avoid it.

THE FRAUD

You mean, bin Laden's still alive? Is he really in Iran now? You've actually been working with him behind the scenes, haven't you?

Sensing he'd made a gaffe, apparently, the Fascist immediately distracted off the issue, knowing what would work with lascivious men of any race, creed or nationality.

THE FASCIST

> Never mind all that—he's just a CIA asset anyway. We would never work with such a creature.

> As I was saying, I immensely enjoyed watching a clip showing that one-of-a-kind woman, the one with mountainous breasts, named "Dolly Parton" or some such. She was being asked about Slick Willy's sexual escapades. Smiling with her lovely teeth showing, she said, "He is a horny toad, ain't he?"

The midget dictator roared at his own joke. It was clear to me that the rabid oppression of women in his regime had made locker-room humor an obsession with him, as it had so many others in Islam as a whole.

THE FASCIST

> I just love that. I had to look up that expression, "horny toad," to find out what it meant. That is one of my hobbies: I love to enlarge my repertoire of words, expressions, idioms and whatnot.

THE FRAUD

> That's good. In fact it is admirable that you have such an inquisitive mind. May I call you "Ahi" for short, since Ahmadinejad is such a long tongue-twister? You know we are brothers in faith and equals in rank. So, we can dispense with all formalities and speak to one another as two brothers would. As the old saying goes, *Bayn-ul-ahbab takthar-ul-aadaab*—"Formalities break or have no place between friends." So may I?

I cringed when I heard the Fraud's words, thinking, there he goes with sucking up to foreign despots again. *But it was clear he was conflicted—like millions worldwide, I had to chalk it all up to his real faith. Despite his attempts at diplomacy, the smooth-talker managed to piss off the tyrant, which historically had not been difficult to do, as the Iranian was known to have a quick trigger finger.*

THE FASCIST

> No! You dare not call us "Ahi." You know what "Ahi" means in Farsi? It means "repugnant" or "nauseating." We know that our enemies have called us many worse names. We take those name-callings as compliments. It makes us feel kinship with the beloved Rasul Allah—the Messenger of Allah, whom we call Muhammad (pbuh). Did not the swine Meccans call the beloved, *shaeron majnoon,* the "Crazed Poet?" They could not, with their moronic brains, appreciate the magnificent verses of Allah's Prophet. But, we will be damned if we allow you, *kaka siah,* to call us anything of the sort. And you yourself have been called many names, we are certain.

THE FRAUD

> Yes, you're so right. You yourself just now called me *kaka siah,* which I understand is a pejorative term for blacks. It's Farsi, not Arabic, but I have heard it before from another ass I ran into during my college days at Harvard. It is one of the many epithets that perhaps match and even exceed those attributed to you, such as "zealot," "fascist," "fanatic," "anti-Semite," "lunatic" and more, such as "someone who is in urgent need of psychological help" and "a person out of touch with reality, who represents nothing of substance." Just little stuff like that.

I don't speak Farsi, but it is most fortunate that we both are fluent in Arabic, the language of the Holy Quran. We can—just the two of us without interpreters—speak frankly and avoid misunderstanding. I'm impressed by your excellent command of English. Our CIA boys—those fat-ass Washington desk jockeys—never told me about this. They either didn't know or they tried to sabotage me, per their usual practice.

Anyway, I agree with you about those primitive Meccans and their inability to appreciate the holy verses revealed by Rasul Allah—the Holy Messenger of Allah. Enlighten me, if you will, why it is, then, that a good number of today's topnotch theologians are also unable to make heads or tails out of many of the verses? They even call the Holy Quran "nothing more than nonsensical mumbo-jumbo hallucinations of an illiterate"—Islam's enemies say that. Frankly, between you and me, even I myself—a believer in the sacred text, as you know from my calling it the "Holy Quran"—am unable to understand many of its verses.

These critics raise troubling questions. They cannot accept that the Holy Quran is a divine revelation, word for word the literal words of Allah. They question how Muhammad (pbuh)—who couldn't even read and write—could remember every word exactly as revealed to him in the cave and later dictate them to someone who could write them down! "Was the illiterate Muhammad able to proof-read what the scribes recorded?" they counter. They further bring up the matter that the recorded verses were in fact from numerous people and that Othman, the second Caliph, had them gathered as best he could, tossed out some verses, added other reports, compiled the volume and ordered all other materials destroyed. See how troublesome it is to answer these allegations?

THE FASCIST

Yes, we do see. We see because we have the inner eye—the eye of faith. These detractors are not given the eye of faith. They are in fact here as agents of the S*haytan al-raheem*—the sinister Satan. Their task is to rattle our faith and make us doubt the truth and the magnificence of Allah and His verses.

THE FRAUD

Excellent explanation you just gave—that ought to shut them up. We agree on the beauty of the peaceful Islamic religion. We are here to iron out our differences and work things to our mutual benefit. In this bizarre quest, I have so many questions I don't even know where to start.

THE FASCIST

You should have brought your teleprompter with you, to cue you. You are at a loss without it, are you not? You remind us of another one of your inept presidents, named Gerald Ford. He was reportedly unable to chew gum and walk straight at the same time, not to mention his golf game. A goofball and a true menace he was to the spectators, as he fired off the poor little ball every which way.

Speaking of ball, that reminds me of how Ford got his little brains jarred—playing that savage game you erroneously call "football," when he was in college at Michigan. On one occasion, someone caught him acting like an imbecile, at the level of a six-year-old. You know what his response was? "What do you expect from a Ford? I am not a Cadillac!" He could have

fooled us. We always thought him a horse and
buggy, at best. And by the way, he had an
uncanny resemblance to a horse, do you not
think?

*The two shared a moment of levity before the Fascist
realized that he should not violate the rigid Islamic
ethos that frowns on even smiling and nearly prohibits
laughter altogether. Islam—particularly his Shi'a
Islam—is a creed of sorrow and death. A creed steeped
in guilt and contemptuous of a life of joy, since the
people of Kufeh, over a thousand years ago, failed in
going to the aid of Muhammad's grandson Hussein as
he was slaughtered like a sheep by the forces of
another power contender, Yazid.*

THE FRAUD

Well, yeah, you're funny. I didn't know you had
a sense of humor. Some of your enemies even
say that you don't have any kind of sense at all.
I think they underestimate your intelligence,
or, rather, *cunning.*

We got sidetracked. In any event, I've got one of
many questions, as I said. But this one struck
me and the American public as being very
weird: When you visited New York, someone
challenged you for the way your government
mistreats homosexuals. In an interview, with a
straight face you said that you don't have
homosexuals in Iran! Then tell me, who are
those people you keep hanging in public
squares for the "crime" of homosexuality,
including teenage boys? Boys your mullahs—
clergymen—probably violated in the first place?

THE FASCIST

We still stick to our answer: We don't have
homosexuals in Iran. How? As you say, we
hang them, that is how. If one of our mullahs
has done such a thing, it is because Allah

ordained it. The boy should consider himself lucky. But only the boy is the homosexual, since he is, as you say, the "catcher."

And again violating the Shi'ite etiquette, the deranged elf doubled up with laughter that sounded remarkably like the howling of a hyena—and he looked remarkably like one too.

THE FRAUD

Ugh. I hope you're joking, but I suspect you aren't. I can't tell you how difficult it is for me to sit in your presence, but I did promise this meeting.

Anyway, calm down. You're going to bust a gut, man, and we won't be able to carry on with our business. We haven't even gotten started yet.

You may wonder how is it possible for any one creature such as the creepy Fascist to embody all evil traits known to man as well as some that are not presently known. The answer is the clergy. The vast cadre of rank-and-file wolves of Allah—starting with the village mullahs all the way to the Grand Ayatollahs— pump superstition, hatred and savagery into the brains of their followers from shortly after birth. Creatures like the Fascist are the valedictorians of the Shi'ite Islamic madrassas or schools.

Suddenly, there was a rap on the door, and a Thick Thug sporting the same kind of scraggy whiskers as the Fascist entered the room, bowed to the little guy and reminded him that it was prayer time. The Fascist and the Fraud immediately ended the meeting to pray together facing Mecca, beseeching assistance of Allah for their next meeting, scheduled for after the dictator's habitual afternoon siesta.

Act Two

The two Laurel and Hardy wanabees walked into the extremely small, windowless room, with the Fascist leading the way. I kept wondering why they chose to meet in such cramped quarters. My guess is they wanted the whole thing be hush-hush and secure. The wretched tyrant almost bounced as he walked, itching to slump on his cushion and carry on.

THE FASCIST

> Now, as I was about to say, the big ticket item is Afghanistan. You know, brother, give it up. America cannot win here. Take my advice: Cut your losses, and let us do the job for you at a bargain basement price.

THE FRAUD

> Are you offering me a "fair deal" again? I told you how I feel about people volunteering to give me "fair deals." Now, why do you want to do that? Did you have a vision? Did the Sahib al-Zaman—the Lord of the Age—direct you to be nice to the Great Satan during a recent visit to the well?

As had I, the Fraud had obviously heard the tales about the megalomaniac claiming a powerful invisible entity talks to him, directs him and gives him divine revelation straight from "On High."

The Fascist

Be reverent, brother, and do not speak rudely about the Beloved of the World—and do not ridicule me. I am here to do business, so let us stick to that, okay?

The Fraud

So, we pull American forces out of Afghanistan and contract the job to you. You are going to send your military and Revolutionary Guard across the border and in no time at all you will subdue the Taliban and slaughter every Al-Qaeda fighter?

The Fascist

No, not a single Iranian soldier will cross into Afghanistan. I repeat, not a single one.

The Fraud

Okay, I got it. You go to the well and ask the Sahib al-Zaman to ordain it.

The Fascist

Once again, I am warning you to stop being so impertinent and cease ridiculing my relationship with the Beloved and his supernatural powers. No, we will not involve him in mundane and trivial matters like this. We can, with his unfailing blessings, handle it without a hitch.

The Fraud

Okay, hitch-less it is. I'm listening.

The Fascist

As I told you before, I am going to just sketch the brief outline of our plan. Here is how it is going to work. Better than 10 percent of Afghanis are Shi'a, our religious kinfolk. They are our *true* brothers: They hate the Sunni *kafir*—unbeliever—majority and would jump at a chance of forcing the Sunnis to treat them right. And we would simply help them clean up their country and set it straight.

THE FRAUD

How do you do that? You bus your supporters—if you can find or hire enough of them—to the border and cheer your Afghan brothers to "force" the Sunni *kuffar* or unbelievers to capitulate?

THE FASCIST

Now, that is the kind of strategy which is more likely to come from your big-bottom top brass at the Pentagon. But do not get defensive and try to cover their sedentary huge butts and peanut-size brains. Their records convict them conclusively. No, we will not do that.

What do we do? We take our Afghani fighting brothers across the border. We train them, arm them, finance them and send them back to the job. An old Farsi saying advises, "The lion of the meadow of Mazendaran can be captured by none other than a Mazendarani warrior." Do I have to clarify that for you? After all, your law degree from Harvard ought to help you understand these metaphors, right?

THE FRAUD

You're saying that it's the local boys who are apt to do the job, rather than outsiders like the Americans and their NATO allies, right?

THE FASCIST

Right, and go to the head of the class. And by now America should have learned this lesson through bitter experience of its misadventure in Vietnam and even in Iraq, although Iraq is somewhat quiet for now. But that is not because of the huge funds the U.S. poured down that rat-hole and the tens of thousands of its forces who died and were maimed there.

What seems like a little success right now is due to the work of the local boys themselves with our assistance. Even America's Sunni allies got sick of CIA-front Al-Qaeda's excesses, and we leaned on our proxies to lie low. Believe me, America simply accomplished little more than squandering the lives of its soldiers and over a million Iraqis, and feeding the ever-ravenous American military-industrial complex. Remember, it was *your* hero, American President Dwight Eisenhower, who sounded the alarm about the killer cabal, the military-industrial gang, which assuredly is dominated by Jews.

I was stunned to hear this rant by the puny tyrant— what did he mean Al-Qaeda was a CIA front? I had not heard that particular conspiracy theory before—first he said that bin Laden was a "CIA asset," now this? And where did he get the figure of 1 million Iraqis killed in the Iraq war? I smelled propaganda out of this weasel's mouth.

THE FRAUD

Wow! Your head is just full of stuff, and the dots you connect lead somewhere, I'm sure. Not a bad job for someone who didn't even go to Harvard Law School. How could a traffic engineer be such a compendium of knowledge and dazzling intellect?

THE FASCIST

Although we cannot be sure, we will take that as a compliment. Now, where were we? Oh yes, we want to assure you that we can deliver what we promise. We have staying power and are determined to do what it takes to accomplish what we set out to do. When we say that we can do the job for you here in Afghanistan, we can back it up. We defeated the perfidious heretic Saddam Hussein, the butcher of Baghdad with all the Arab countries supporting him. Not to mention that the United States supplied him with intelligence, poison gas and all kinds of weapons to kill our brave warriors by the thousands. Do you think that we have forgotten America's role in that war, which killed so many of our Shi'a brethren? We may look friendlier to you today, but we have a long memory—the Great Satan's apologists and citizens just do not realize that Allah's true Muslims have serious, legitimate grievances that they aim to redress.

That animal Donald Rumsfeld personally visited Saddam and brokered all kinds of deals with him against us. How we wish we could get our hands on that pompous criminal.

THE FRAUD

Okay, okay. I can see why you hate America so much for supporting the Shah, for siding with Iraq and so forth. What I don't understand is your rabid support for the Arab cause, in spite of the fact that you just told me how they all rallied behind Saddam against you. You ought to know when crunch time comes again the Arabs will gang up on you Iranians once more. Maybe the Shah was more realistic befriending Israel and getting some backing from them against their perennial common enemy, the Arabs. How do you answer that?

THE FASCIST

It is simplicity itself, as Sherlock Holmes liked to say. We do not give a pig's snout for the Arabs. For that matter, we do not give a mouse's tail for Iran either. That stumping for the Arab cause is just a ruse. We the Shi'a, the true Muslims, are only 10 percent, while the Sunnis are the other 90 percent. Our ultimate aim is to do whatever we must to wrestle the mantle of leadership from the Sunnis and bring them under the tabernacle of the Sahib al-Zaman. Get it? First we herd in the treacherous Sunni Muslims, then the rest of the *kafir* world.

THE FRAUD

As we knew you were—because you continually spy on everybody, persecuting and punishing all those who step outside of your box of oppression—you are very knowledgeable about a wide variety of subjects, so I'll continue to pick your brain.

THE FASCIST

Feel free to ask whatever you want, and we will try, with the aid of Allah, to answer your questions and dispel your perplexities.

There was a clearly discernible change in the Fascist, as he swallowed the pounds of grease applied to him by the Fraud. The pompous despot began using the word nahno—*"we," in the royal sense, much more frequently instead of* ana—*"I"—and assumed an air of great superiority. Then again, for the rest of the meeting, forgetting his pretentiousness, he would switch back and forth confusedly between his delusional "royal we" and his insignificant "I."*

Act Three

*O*nce again, the ritualistic exchange of Islamic greeting in Arabic and three pecks on each cheek, after which the two egomaniacs got down to business. As I watched, I thought to myself that there was no more compelling evidence of the sorry condition of the world than the fact that these two loonies wield enough power to end it. The Fascist seemed itching to fire the opening salvo and, by so doing, assume the high ground.

THE FASCIST

Listen up, and listen up good. You—I mean, *America*, of course—are going bust. Your government is just like your people. You all live way beyond your means. Your people go bankrupt by the millions because they get to the point that not even your loan-shark banks lend them any money. So, they lose their cars, homes and even their household furniture to the repo and foreclosure vulture—

THE FRAUD

I take it you're trying to rub it in, as if I am responsible? Come on, man, tell me something I don't know. Why are you wasting our time talking about this? A man who lives beyond his means must end up facing the music. That's not unique to America—it's the same all over the world. Don't you read the economic reports of credible institutions such as the World Bank? You know what they say? They say there isn't enough money in the world—

THE FASCIST

Patience, patience, my dear brother. Remember: *Allahoma yejazzi al saaberoon be ajron men gheyre* hesaab—"Allah compensates the patient ones with infinite rewards"—is a saying attributed to the blessed lips of the beloved Messenger Rasul Allah. So, be patient, brother. For now, let us leave it at saying that the problem is complex, and allow me to tell you what relevance it has to our discourse.

The U.S. government also keeps borrowing money and spending like a drunken sailor. Between the Arab oil peddlers and the Chinese trinket sellers, they own you. They own shiploads of your nearly worthless treasury bonds. The Chinese have hoarded so much of it that they have started squawking publicly. They have threatened to dump the stuff, much less buy any more of it. The way you are going, your two little girls and the coming generations of Americans will be taking in laundry for the Chinese. The shoe will be on the other foot, so to speak.

THE FRAUD

Yeah, yeah. Stop worrying about my watch, brother. You have so many of your own problems that you hardly need to use your Einstein brains to solve ours—

THE FASCIST

Stop right there. First you want to call me "Ahi," which means "repulsive." Now you befoul my brains by connecting them to that dumb-ass Jew who had nothing original to contribute, yet he stole other people's work and claimed it as his own. A typical Jew, I say. That moron could not hack primary school, remember? All of a sudden he became the genius of the age? How did he do it? By craftily stealing other people's work and claiming it as his own, I say. Jews, Jews, Jews. The Best Beloved of Allah, the one-and-only true Messenger, recognized the Jews for what they are and dealt with them with the justice of Allah in Medina, where our Holy Prophet (saw) executed 700 men of the Jewish Banu Qurayza tribe. That is why we, His faithful, are duty-bound to complete the work that the Prophet himself pursued: We must cleanse Allah's earth from the microbes of Jews. We must destroy Israel utterly.

THE FRAUD

Like they say, a true anti-Semite. Tell me if you would: Why, then, did the Holy Prophet (saw), with his infinite power, let the Jews thrive? According to the Holy Quran and the commentaries, Muhammad (pbuh) split the moon with one slash of his sword and performed many other miracles, didn't he? I don't mean to sound skeptical, I am just curious.

THE FASCIST

Look, if the Messenger of Allah had exterminated *all* the Jews, then how could his adoring followers earn merit points, merit points that we need for admission into Paradise? Out of his infinite kindness, Rasul Allah left us a great deal of work. Can you not appreciate that?

But see here—you too are a Jew-hater, aren't you?

THE FRAUD

Some people say so, and I guess I don't give off a good impression when I so blatantly suck up to other members of the Ummah, the global Muslim community—I suppose I should tone that down. I'm doing my best to help out our oppressed Palestinian brethren—did you hear about me snubbing the Israeli Prime Minister Benjamin Netanyahu when he came to the White House? I think that should show them a thing or two, as it did when I made that comment about journalist Danny Pearl's beheading. I said, "Obviously, the loss of Daniel Pearl was one of those moments that captured the world's imagination because it reminded us of how valuable a free press is." My critics were quick to point out that Pearl was a Jew and was murdered because of that fact, so my remark looks quite trite and insensitive.

I'm really trying to make Islam look not so bad. But you guys aren't helping—all the suicide bombings, beheadings and indiscriminate killings are giving Islam a really bad reputation. Since 9/11, there have been over 15,000 fatal Islamist terrorist attacks globally!

Nevertheless, I apologize for connecting you in any way to that crafty Jew Einstein—you have no idea what influences I am under. I've got to deal with the bad rep of Islam, as well as having powerful Zionists breathing down my neck all day long. But we can't have *your* solution to the "Jewish problem." The difference between us is that you blare out your hatred without being able to do much more than make life a living hell for the few Jews still remaining in Iran. If I did that, the American Zionists would lynch me. You know, lynching blacks used to be a favorite pastime activity in America. There are some who are still nostalgic about those years and want to bring the practice back.

THE FASCIST

First of all, as concerns who did 9/11, the Muslim Ummah only claims responsibility when it is convenient to rally the troops and uplift morale. At those times, we refer to the alleged suicide bombers as "The Magnificent 19 Martyrs." Otherwise, publically we uncategorically deny that Muslims had anything to do with 9/11, which we then say was an "inside job" carried out by the CIA and the Mossad. We are so fortunate that Allah commands us to speak out of both sides of our mouths, as you Yanks say, especially when it comes to the stupid infidels, who are so easy to fool!

We lie to the dumb *kuffar* all the time, including in describing the true Ummah. When it is convenient for us Shi'a brethren, we loudly trumpet the fact that there are 1.5 billion Muslims worldwide, but when it is also convenient for us, we dismiss the 90 percent of Sunnis as heretics, *kuffar* and infidels.

And, by the way, do you know why the date of 9/11 was chosen? Because of the scripture in our Holy Quran, *ayah* 9:111, which guarantees us a seat in Paradise for killing infidels:

"Allah has bought from the believers their lives and worldly wealth, and in return has promised them the Garden (of Paradise). They will fight for the cause of Allah, and will slay and be slain."

Regarding your other comments, yes, you do go around the world and expose the evil-doings of the American administration, controlled by the twin evils of Wall Street and Zionists. Actually they are one and the same, since the Jews own Wall Street as well. But 9/11 really took care of that, did it not? It cost the American economy billions of dollars, which pleased us greatly.

In any event, apology accepted—back to what I was proposing. What I am doing, in the spirit of Islamic charity from one brother to another, is helping you out to save the broke and broken American nation. Do I need to tell you that even your Golden State, California—the engine of your soon-to-be-wrecked-train—is flat broke? It is short $19 billion this year alone. It is so sad that it is hilarious. It is a comedy, I say. California turns to your Federal government, hat in hand for a handout, while you kiss up to the Chinese and the Arabs to loan you some more money. Then your people have the gall to call *me* zany. Who is really zany, tell me?

THE FRAUD

You're so full of crap, your eyes are brown. So, the Mossad—the Jews—did 9/11, which destroyed their own financial district, costing them billions? That makes no sense at all. Maybe some Jews were involved—and there could've been some of just about any group on the planet involved at some level, including Muslims. But we don't even want to go there, brother, because we aren't really at the top of the food chain, are we?

Anyway, I'm impressed—how do you know all this? You even knew what Dolly said about Slick Willy being a horny toad. Your public image and what the CIA paints of you are so vastly different from what I see myself. They think you are a glib, head-in-the-sand, two-bit-jerk who houses nothing more than crap in his cranium. I mean, *I* don't say that—that 's what your public image is. Now, I can see that they are dead wrong. That's why a *tête-à-tête* like the one we are having is so critical at getting to the real skinny.

THE FASCIST

What is the "real skinny?" We know all the important stuff, but we do not usually bother with the kind of street slang that you have acquired in the course of wading your way through the slums of Chicago and the cesspool of the Chicago Democratic Party.

THE FRAUD

All right, knock off the abusive language. But you're wise not to bother with street slang, because it can be a waste of gray matter. Now that you asked, the "real skinny" means the "real scoop."

THE FASCIST

The "real poop," did you say?

THE FRAUD

I see you just can't resist the street humor after all. In fact, I'm quite sure you are amused by it. Anyway, the real skinny, real scoop and real poop all mean the same thing. The English language is so vast—the unabridged dictionary lists nearly one million words. Not like Farsi where you can't say two words without one of them being Arabic. From what I've understand, most Arab-speakers can't understand the classical Arabic of the Quran, and regional dialects vary so much that it's difficult for two Arabic speakers from different parts of the Arab world to communicate with each other.

THE FASCIST

Yes, yes, that is true. But Farsi? My arsie! Who gives a rat's hindquarter for Farsi? Farsi and anything non-Islamic or pre-Islamic are all trash, I say. It is Arabic, the language of revelation, which counts. And yes, yes, you are correct—in due time, we shall toss that 1,000,000-word English and all other languages in the dustpan where they belong, and have Arabic as the common and only tongue. That day is coming. Count on it. As we say, "Arabic only by 2030."

And for your one-million-word English language, that reminds me of the blessed words of the Messenger of Allah where he says, *Al elmo nughtatan katharho al jaaheloon*—"Knowledge is but a dot, expanded by ignorant people."

THE FRAUD

Surely the blessed Prophet (pbuh) must've been using a metaphor. How could knowledge be only a dot? And of all people, how could *ignorant* people expand it?

THE FASCIST

That is the difference between true believers like me and chameleons like you. To me, every word that has issued forth from his blessed lips is a literal truth. The Messenger of Allah needs not rely upon banalities of metaphor, allegories and similes.

THE FRAUD

I love Arabic, as you know, but all these facts remind me that I don't want my grandchildren to speak *only* Arabic, which is a plank in the Muslim Brotherhood agenda to Islamize the world—

THE FASCIST

Ugh. The Muslim Brotherhood! Those *kuffar* infidels are nothing but puppets of the CIA and the Mossad. We will fight them too, as they are just Zionist agents.

The Fraud

Well, some might say that's an outrageous claim, to say the least. But I hear so many, and nothing surprises me. If all of it were true, I'd have to say that the SuperJews who omnipotently run *everything* must be superior indeed. They can so easily make complete fools of the Egyptians, Arabs and Sunnis in general by being behind the Muslim Brotherhood?! Perhaps you've forgotten who a number of my major supporters have been? And if the SuperJews control everything in the world, who do *you* work for?

Anyway, we've got pressing problems in the here and now that we need to work out between us. In our mutual love for Islam, we are two brothers, but we represent diametrically different positions. I mean, I am the President of America, and you are the President of the Islamic Republic of Iran, and the countries we represent have been at loggerheads for many years. What we need to do is to have a private understanding of working together towards furthering the Ummah and publicly pretend that we are still irreconcilable enemies, although personally I'm not pretending, because you really are disgusting. But to make this play, we need to keep up a degree of hostility for public consumption—a sort of shadow boxing, if you know what I mean.

The Fascist

Please do not even suggest that we personally are under the control of the "SuperJews," as you put it. We are being advised from On High, far above the long reach of the Zionist arm— and that is precisely why you need to join us.

We—the truth believers, of which you too can and must become one—must time and again thank Rasul Allah for giving us all the tools and instructions we need to implement *his* design, not that of any "SuperJews." As you know, an indispensable powerful tool at our disposal is *taqiyya*—lying—ordained by Muhammad (pbuh) himself. *Taqiyya* frees us completely from having to be stymied by any commitment, it allows us to say one thing and do the opposite if it suits us, and clearly puts our adversary at a disadvantage. And that is the way it should be. The work of Allah must be implemented, following His guidelines, and none of the trashy standards made up by infidels should get in the way.

Once more, a rap on the door is followed by the appearance of the Thick Thug, who informs their Excellencies that the afternoon prayer time was at hand. Showing his great respect for Islam, which he had proved many times, the Fraud joined his "brother" in spreading their prayer rugs, facing Mecca and performing their prayers, anxious to get the five-times-a day bother out of the way and get on with their important business.

Act Four

By now, observing the ritual of hugs between the small Fascist and his towering counterpart began to turn my stomach. The terrorist-funder could barely clear the privates of the purported Christian convert, much less reach his face to smack his filthy foaming lips on the latter's reluctant cheeks. And the Fraud— the master bower-gesticulator, per his usual habit of pandering to high authority—would deferentially bend to his knees to grant the little fellow the pecks and to reciprocate. It was difficult to tell whether the taller man was enjoying or just tolerating the ritual. He certainly didn't want to appear he was enjoying the contact by the Fascist, being acutely aware of the murderous tyrant's stance on anything that might smack of homosexuality, even though the ugly troll himself engaged in kissing men on the mouth and assorted other practices that could be construed as homoerotic. But, perhaps it was the thought of that thick yahoo, noose in hand, escorting him to the nearest tree limb or a lamppost that was giving the Fraud the willies, since he was trembling visibly during the "coupling."

Once again, the Fascist polluted the atmosphere with his squeaky, condescending voice.

THE FASCIST

We have been exercising considerable patience in fending off the machinations of American agents, most of whom, if not all, are clearly Zionist provocateurs—

THE FRAUD

Hold off, hold off, brother. Did you have a bad night? Did your *manzel*—your "old lady," or what you call your "house"—give you a bad time? Why are you starting our meeting with such rancor?

THE FASCIST

First of all, it is impudent of you to inquire about my house. She is none of your concern or anyone else's concern, for that matter. Besides, none of my houses dares to give me a bad time. I am the one in charge of them. Their duty, as clearly stipulated by the Messenger of Allah, is to be obedient and subservient to their husbands. His Blessedness ordains in the Holy Quran, *Al rejaalo ghavaamoone ala al nesa*— "Men are rulers over women"—as you should well know.

Secondly, I just about never take a *manzel* with me when I travel. No need. Anytime I feel the urge to discharge, a *sigheh*—a temporary wife that we pious men may marry for any length of time, from a few hours or for as long as we wish—is provided for me by my attendants.

THE FRAUD

Yes, I do know about how you fanatics treat women. Beating, hanging and stoning girls who are raped? Remember the stoning of Soraya M.? The Iranian penal code allows you to bury women deeper than men so there is no chance for them to escape. How am I supposed to go along with such atrocity and human-rights violations?

THE FASCIST

Yours is not to question the Holy Quran and Sharia law. You just accept these ordinances from On High. Islam is the best thing that has ever happened to man—all we men have to do is to be devoted followers of the blessed Messenger, and we reap the rewards. One of them is Rasul Allah's ordaining four concurrent wives for a man—although he himself reportedly had at least 15, not counting the numerous slave women he kept. But, again that is what really set him aside from ordinary men, is it not? Satisfying the carnal needs of 15 women truly requires a supernatural personage. And this is one of many proofs of his uniqueness.

Knowing full well that we mortals will never be able to match his prowess, the Holy Prophet (saw) has allowed us four wives and as many *sigheh* as we can handle. Blessed be his soul, our beloved Messenger. Yet, uppity women and even some men think this provision to be misogynistic, since no *woman* is allowed such privileges.

Yes, yes indeed. It is incredible that these louts have the impudence to question the Messenger's commandment! The fact is that Islam is the *perfect* religion for men. If you want a better religion than the faith of Allah, you have to make it up yourself.

THE FRAUD

Ahsan, *ahsan*—excellent, excellent, well put. Interesting you say that, if you want a better religion you have to make it up yourself. One of the many disrespectful things non-Muslims say is that Muhammad (pbuh) did just that, in order to satisfy his lust for sex and power.

Your own mullahs seize "immoral" girls off streets and turn them into sex slaves in their government-regulated brothels. These numerous brothels provide "temporary marriages" (*mutah*) for male pilgrims to holy sites who need to be serviced. But critics say your women-oppression doesn't end there, as Iran's "holy" regime engages in the *global* sex-slave trade as well, kidnapping girls and selling them to the Arab world. And what about all the girls murdered after they've been raped and forced into prostitution? Many of these victimized and abused girls were pregnant from the rapists.

Does the name Atefeh Rajabi Sahaaleh ring a bell? Your government was forced to act only after international outcry, but still this 16-year-old girl's rapist and executioner—a judge!—was not brought to justice.

How about Taraneh Mousavi, the beautiful 19-year-old girl with green eyes who was kidnapped by members of your Basij team—the volunteer militia founded by Ayatollah Khomeini—who tortured, raped and sodomized her repeatedly until she became unconscious? Your Basij dogs gang-raped her and then burned her body, after stealing it from the hospital, where she died from the brutal injuries the scum inflicted upon her.

There are just too many of these atrocities to name—as you know, according to Iranian sharia law, no virgin girl is allowed to be executed, so your thugs just rape them first. Brother, you are making my life very difficult—I still have to answer to the American people, and, unlike you, I actually have a conscience.

From the looks of it, critics claim, Islam itself was designed as little more than a means of enslaving women for sex, baby-making and

housework—how am I supposed to answer all
these criticisms and critics?

*My stomach churned at these horrible stories, which I
vividly recalled with horror, and I wanted to strangle
the murderous Islamist bastard with my own bare
hands. Anyway, the American's last comment set the
Fascist off on a typical inflammatory rant that deflected
away from his terrible guilt.*

THE FASCIST

I would like nothing better than to cut their
tongues off, the impious and blasphemous
scumbags of whom you speak.

*As the hours wore on—and it was rather tedious
watching these tapes, because these two men
interspersed their dreadful conversations with odd
personal habits such as picking their noses and
expelling gas, which I found to be juvenile—I noticed
that the Fraud seemed to be speaking more like the
Fascist, as if he were imbibing some of the latter's
religious delusions of grandeur and megalomania, as
well as his accent and other cultural attributes. I was
also reminded that the American was a social
chameleon—a rainbow child, some believed—who could
move easily among a variety of company. An admirable
quality in many cases, but it sickened me here.*

THE FRAUD

Brother, you know what else these critics say?
For one, they cite the case of the Jewess
Rihana, the most beautiful woman of Banu
Qurayza tribe. Muhammad (pbuh) had
Rihana's husband and hundreds of other
Jewish captives beheaded and took Rihana
that very night as his newest wife—in other
words, he killed her husband and then turned
her into a sex slave. Unfortunately, they
document this episode from our very own
historical records.

THE FASCIST

These infidel disrespecters of the Prophet (saw) are swine, indeed. Why do you say "unfortunately?" What Rasul Allah is supposed to do with her? Her husband was dead, and the benevolent Muhammad (pbuh) gave the woman a home and a husband no less than himself—Allah's chosen emissary. Ungrateful are these infidels who cannot see Rasul Allah's kindness! It goes to prove that no act of kindness ever goes unpunished. I clearly see the machinations of the Jews in all these blasphemous allegations and distortions of our holy faith.

THE FRAUD

Do you know how the nonbelievers respond to that logic? They say: "Weren't there hundreds of *other* widowed Jewesses? How come Rasul Allah found mercy in his heart for the *most beautiful* woman of her tribe, Rihana, and for none of the others?" Yet, the more I think of it, you may be right with your explanation, as I have quite a chronicle of Zionist schemes.

THE FASCIST

Post them to me later, every last one of them. They delight my heart to hear them and read about them. For now, share with me one or two instances to lift my spirit.

THE FRAUD

Glad to comply. Just one instance will do for now, since we don't want to stray too far from the task at hand...

THE FASCIST

No, no and no. It is important that we feel free to speak about anything that comes to us and not to worry about sticking to business. Keep in mind that when we face the most blessed spot on earth, the *Ka'aba* at Mecca, prostate ourselves in humility to Allah, His Apostle and the Imams, we become like hollow reeds— vehicles for discussing and doing what is channeled through us. We must exercise self-abnegation, get out of the way and allow the hand of Allah to operate. So, speak up.

THE FRAUD

Look, I'm not sure I should encourage you in your Jew-hatred, but I have some personal experiences that didn't make me too happy. Such as, during my Presidential election, Joe Lieberman, a life-long Democratic senator and conservative Jew, bolts the party and starts campaigning for John McCain! Can you believe that?

He evidently feared that I'm a crypto-Muslim, a stealth jihadist, a Manchurian Candidate, and, as such, I'm a devoted follower of Allah and a sworn enemy of the Jews. Of course, I deny it. Joe apparently thought that I would do all that is in my power to undermine the state of Israel and to excise it from Palestine, as Islamists would like to see. To this day, this guy does everything he can to harass me and will see to it that I will not get re-elected.

THE FASCIST

You mean, the *illegitimate* state of Israel, which we should wipe off the face of the earth... But I deny that we are building nuclear weapons with our enriched uranium to do the job.

In any case, nothing you tell me about Jews surprises me. But what I am going to share with you about them ought to enlighten you regarding their true nature. Our beloved Supreme Jurist, Ayatollah Seyyed Ali Khamenei, disclosed to me in a private audience a most remarkable missive he received from On High about the Jews.

His Eminence confided in me that the problem of the Jews befuddled him for decades. Before assuming his awesome task, he had some free time, so he decided to seclude himself in one of the chambers at the shrine of the Sayed Al Shohada—Imam Hussein—in Karbala, and beseech the Imam for the answer to the riddle of the Jews. After praying and fasting for 40 days, one night in a twilight state the Imam appeared to him in person and honored his request.

Without going into details, this is what the Imam told his own dear descendant, his Eminence Seyyed Ali. He told him that Jews are in reality agents of the S*haytan al-raheem*— the sinister Satan—although they appear like ordinary people. And it has been in Allah's plan all along to eliminate them through a gradual process. It was for this reason that Allah had directed the Pharaohs, without the Pharaohs themselves being consciously aware, to kill all first-born Jewish males. Then the Romans did a fairly good job of killing and dispersing them. It was the perfidious Cyrus, the disgraceful king of Persia, who worked against the will of Allah. In the Jewish Book, he is portrayed as the "Messiah" because he supposedly freed the Jews from captivity, helping them return to Palestine and re-build their temple. But *yad-ul-allah foghe aydihom*—"the hand of Allah is supreme to all hands," as the scriptures so rightly proclaim. Allah put an end to the house of Cyrus in punishment for his criminal deed. Then Allah commissioned the Blessed Messenger with the task, and we will complete it.

I shuddered at his genocidal plot, but I noticed how the foul wretch left out Hitler from the list of Allah's major

Jew-killers. Was that an oversight? Not a chance. This sociopath reveres Hitler as much as his other idols. Perhaps knowing full well that the syphilitic Nazi also had blacks on his hit list, the conniver did not want to remind the Fraud about him.

On the other hand, maybe he just didn't want to bring up the Jewish holocaust, which he ferociously denied in the first place. Maybe he could see a paradox in saying that the Jews made up the Holocaust, but that Allah was in fact interested in their systematic destruction in very much the same evil manner.

THE FRAUD

> Your genocidal plot doesn't stand a chance of success. Blowing up Israel doesn't wipe them all out—there are Jews all over the world. For one, there are more Jews in America than in Israel—I should know, as 33 percent of the U.S. Supreme Court is now Jewish.

THE FASCIST

> Yes, the U.S. is truly Jew-ridden. But, why do you think our devoted scientists and engineers are working around the clock making intercontinental missiles? We do not intend to store them. They are indispensable instruments not only for ending the Jewish problem once and for all, but also for triggering Armageddon, if we need to, in order to hasten the advent of the long-prayed-for Sahib al-Zaman—the Twelfth Imam—to return to assume his glorious reign. But, we don't plan to start the fireworks the minute we have produced enough firecrackers. We need them only in case other strategies fail. Otherwise, we know they will destroy the earth, and we have big plans for the planet once we have achieved global domination. If we had neutron bombs, we could use those— just get rid of the infidels and keep their cities. But then, who would do the slave labor?

THE FRAUD

> Are you serious about using the firecrackers at some point? Is this *your* plan, or is it that of the Supreme Leader Khamenei? I know that the Revolutionary Guard is in charge of your nuclear program. What about the regular military? Are they also in on this plot for global domination?

THE FASCIST

> Obviously, you do not know anything about the military. To enlighten you, the duty of the military is to execute orders, not to question them. The Supreme Jurist is the Commander-in-Chief, like the way you are. Except that you wet your pants even thinking about such a possibility, whereas his Eminence do not hesitate a moment if the need arises, and the rest of us, his devoted slaves, will happily carry out his orders. But please do not worry. As I said, this whole thing is precautionary. A sort of thing that may have to be done when all other measures are either exhausted or prove to be ineffective, I assure you. You have my word on it.

On this heart-warming note, they broke to pray. After all, when you are charged with the awesome work of Allah you need to supplicate him earnestly for assistance.

Act Five

*P*rayers out of the way, the meeting resumed. By this time, the two psychological basket-cases felt no compunctions whatsoever about raising any issue, in context or not. They also loosened up considerably at adhering to grammatically correct usages of words and sentences. And it was mostly the Fraud who jumped from topic to topic while the Fascist tried his level best to score points. Out of kindness, henceforth I shall spare you describing the sickening ritual of kiss and hug that invariably took place at the start of each session.

THE FRAUD

> During prayers, something popped into my head that I can't shake off. You mind if I ask you about it and get it out of the way?

THE FASCIST

> Not at all. Go ahead.

THE FRAUD

> You've explained your Shi'ite rationale for dealing harshly with the Jews. But, why is it that you and your group are after the sect of the Baha'is? I really don't know much about them personally other than that they have a beautiful temple outside of Chicago and that they let people of all religions and races visit

there. I once went there and quickly perused some of their beliefs and photos they have posted on the walls. They all seemed peaceful, accepting and nice—

THE FASCIST

You need not teach me about them, since you already admitted that you do not know much about them anyway—

THE FRAUD

Hold your horses, man. You can't tell me one minute I can ask all questions I have and then cut me off. Just zip up a minute, and let me say my peace, okay?

As I was saying, I was impressed. Not only did they seem to advocate all kinds of great ideas such as equality for all people, even genders, and so forth, but they also had a chart on the wall that I think was something about what they call "progressive revelation" or some such. But the thing that really impressed me was they had Muhammad (pbuh) prominently in a list along with Moses, Jesus and finally their own prophet, Bahá'u'lláh. I asked one of the ushers there about that. a young black woman volunteer, who said that they revere Rasul Allah as much as they revere their own prophet. She further said that she herself, born and raised Christian, had to accept Muhammad (pbuh) as a legitimate prophet before the Baha'is would accept her as a member. They were very respectful to the Muslim faith, brother.

THE FASCIST

You finished? Believe me we have looked into it most thoroughly. Once again, I have it from our highest religious divines: These Baha'is are another version of the Jews that Satan has created. But, Satan being the dumb-ass he is, he was not smart enough to avoid making one of his many bad mistakes. Of course, he made his stupidest mistake by contesting Allah. But that was not his only mistake. And I am not going to go into enumerating his mistakes and evil doings. What was his mistake in the case of this new version of the Jews, you ask?

He made their headquarters in the occupied Palestine. Why did he do that? Because he knew very well that devotees of Allah like us would decimate them in no time, and only under the protection of the satanic Zionist can the Baha'is hope to survive and try to subvert the faith of Allah by sending their spies and subversives to every corner of the globe. These subversives take the agenda of the criminal Satan to people of the world and convert them. They still have a large community in Iran, and we are seeing to it that we destroy them in every possible way.

THE FRAUD

I disagree with you in labeling *everyone* "satanic." Are you saying *only* Muslims can be righteous and godly? I heard these things in Indonesia, and some clergymen say the Holy Quran itself prohibits friendships between Muslims and infidels, including the People of the Book, the Jews and Christians.

But we can put that aside for now, as it is a distraction. And there are endless distractions in this world, and we need to stick with important main issues.

THE FASCIST

Of course, the filthy infidels are *all* satanic— you cannot be a true believer if you do not accept that holy fact. But, yes, I agree: We did get sidetracked from our earlier discussion regarding Afghanistan, although we know that the American invasion of that part of Dar al-Islam—the house of Islam—was orchestrated by the Jews too, so even that subject is relevant.

In any event, I told you in a summary form what we are proposing, but did not get a chance to tell you what our contracting the job costs you. And as the President of the United States of America, you need to know and agree, right?

THE FRAUD

Right, go ahead and tell me.

THE FASCIST

I believe I did mention that the deal we are offering you is even below bargain basement prices...

THE FRAUD

I believe you did. And I believe I told you that I hate good deals. Again, you remind me of that sleazy used-car salesman trying to sell my grannie shoddy goods, and I recoil. Go ahead— never mind the good deal and just tell me what it is going to cost.

THE FASCIST

Pocket change, compared to what it is costing you now. We want a few things in exchange, of course. First, you leave us alone to keep working on our nuclear program. If it is good for America, Russia, China, France and even the occupiers of Palestine to have nuclear weapons, why are we being singled out for exclusion? I did not even give a complete list of nations possessing them, and you act like it is their birthright and not ours. Only when it comes to us, you are dead set against us having a few of our own—

THE FRAUD

Of course, because the American allies in the region are sure that you aim to rule the Middle East with your nuclear weapons, while the non-Muslim world is sure that, with the twin life-and-death means of oil and nukes, you will venture out to Islamize the entire world.

And by the way, would you stop saying "you," "you" and more "you?" You are using "you," meaning me, interchangeably with America.

THE FASCIST

Yes, but, last time I checked, you were the President of the Great Satan. That makes you one and the same in my book, although I do know what you mean, because you are an *internationalist* member of the Ummah, are you not?

THE FRAUD

I'm not going to answer that question, as it will incriminate me and give you the opportunity to blackmail me.

THE FASCIST

Yes, yes, sure, sure, but we already have that opportunity. Anyway, as I was saying, that is one big bone you have to throw our way. Another one is that sanction crap—all it does is make life more profitable for contraband runners and black market profiteers. And some of your more hothead hawks keep pushing you to clamp embargoes on us. Can you believe that? Who in the hell is America to even contemplate such an act of piracy? That is what it is, ain't it, as Dolly would say?

THE FRAUD

So, what do you want?

THE FASCIST

We need weapons and spare parts. The spare parts are for all the airplanes, tanks, armored vehicles and whatnot America sold the Shah— and not exactly at bargain basement prices. Those mamas are becoming antiques, and we need the parts to hand off some of the stuff— but not the planes—to our brothers here.

THE FRAUD

Anything else? Your shopping list is getting longer and longer. What are you trying to do, scuttle the deal?

THE FASCIST

Just one more thing. We are chronically short of foodstuffs: Things like wheat that Americans grow in abundance and all kinds of things that can fill a man's belly. We want you to keep us in a steady supply of all stuff that you always have in surplus and that we are chronically short of. We will not be hogging it all ourselves. We would channel much of it to our fighting brethren here who cannot be farming to feed their families and fighting at the same time. And no man can fight on an empty stomach.

THE FRAUD

Except for the nuclear stuff, the other demands seem reasonable and possibly doable. Speaking of not being able to fight on an empty stomach, my stomach just signaled that it can't go on without refueling. So, what do you say we break for a bite?

Act Six

After having had a bite that lasted over an hour, the two full-stomached, empty-headed clowns got back to work generating clearly audible sounds from their upper as well as lower orifices.

THE FASCIST

Are we on the same page on the deal, our contract?

THE FRAUD

You know that the deal is not completely up to me. Not by a long shot. Sure, I have to like it to get it rolling. But, at the very least I have to get the consent of Congressional leaderships. I'll get back to you on that as soon as we work it out. I'm not making any promises, mind you, particularly about the nuclear thing. It is an awfully touchy issue, since "you know who"— the people who really run everything—are deadly opposed to letting you have a few of the toys we and others have.

THE FASCIST

I am a reasonable man. I understand. But, you must give me your word that you'll push for it as hard as you can. It is really vital to us and our plans. I must say that at least we are making progress and developing understanding between us. Critical, however, for executing our sacred mission of setting aright the crooked path of the present world is that we share the same belief, albeit you are still a heretic—and an apostate, at least in the eyes of many devout Muslims.

THE FRAUD

You know that in my heart I have always loved Islam, the great faith of my childhood. I have tremendous respect for the Holy Prophet (saw) and Holy Quran.

THE FASCIST

Being a Muslim and a devotee of Rasul Allah in your heart is good, but not good enough. One has to take two additional vital steps: A step *away* from the tainted Sunni belief perpetrated by the traitorous Caliphs and another step *towards* entering under the true tabernacle of Rasul Allah's house.

THE FRAUD

Okay, okay—spell it out for me, please.

THE FASCIST

Spell what out? Rasul Allah? R-A-S—

THE FRAUD

No, no. "Spell it out" is a way of requesting clarification.

THE FASCIST

All right. We mean true Islam is the Shi'a Islam. It is the pure blood of Rasul Allah that courses in the veins of his descendants and thus makes them worthy of leading his Ummah. Not the conniving power-hungry Caliphs who prevented Imam Ali, Rasul Allah's cousin and son-in-law, from assuming the mantle of leadership for the Ummah. That unforgivable treachery has been the cause of great suffering for Muslims and a huge setback for Islam's progress.

THE FRAUD

My Sunni friends would probably say in turn that you and the Shi'ite ayatollahs, mullahs, imams and the rest are full of crap, because there is no way in the world that they are descended from Muhammad (pbuh). They'd say that the story about Imam Zaman Madhi and the well is pure baloney made up by the clergy to justify its existence and give itself power.

THE FASCIST

All right, never mind all the sacrilege. We do not have much time together.

At the risk of regressing, we need to elaborate for you our earlier effort. We hope you bear with us. We wrote to that big mouth, no-good-alcoholic Texan—you know who. We do not want to mention him by name. We invited him to embrace the true faith. Of course, he spurned the best offer of his disgraceful life, that murderer of many thousands. But, you have a chance to shed your apostasy and to accept the summons to embrace the great faith—

THE FRAUD

The reality is that I have done immense service to the holy Islamic faith. Didn't your people show you the text of my speeches in Cairo and Turkey? How I praised Islam like few "Westerners" ever have, even making a number of contentions not supported by history? Have you not noticed how at every opportunity I speak glowingly of Islam, the Holy Quran and the priceless contribution of Islam to the world? Didn't I basically put an end to the lie that the United States is a "Christian" nation?

Didn't I say publicly that I hail from a Muslim
family, including not only my father but also
my very own brothers, and that the sound of
adhan—the Muslim call to prayer—is the most
beautiful sound in the world? Didn't I order
that no one in my government should use the
word "jihadist" to describe America's enemies,
because the word slanders the sacred concept
of jihad—the Islamic struggle against vice and
unbelief—and by so saying makes terrorists of
those devoted servants of Allah?

Didn't I also forbid our national security
agencies from even mentioning Islam in their
reports on terror? Didn't the investigative
committee publish its report on the Fort Hood
shootings without mentioning Islam? My
devotion to Islam is thoroughly on record.

And as for this Christian veneer I have been
wearing, it is simply to help me rise to a
position of power, where I can be most effective
in helping further the goals of the Ummah
toward world peace. As you know, the church I
attended was a forum more for exposing and
vilifying the Jew-run America than for
preaching Christianity. The church itself was
claimed to be a great subterfuge for
undermining the sworn enemies of Islam, the
Zionists and the Christian fanatics. That
scandal almost destroyed my career—

The Fascist

Yes, you can stop now. As you say, let me spell
it out for you, even running the risk of
repeating myself. We do not consider Sunnis to
be Muslims. If you are Muslim, you are a Shi'a.
Sunnis are traitors to the house of Rasul Allah.
The true Islam is Shi'a Islam that follows the
Pure Twelve Imams—the seeds of Muhammad
(pbuh) himself. I am offering you the inestimable

gift of *Shi'a* Islam, and you do well to accept it. Given your lifelong history of shifting quicker than desert sand as situations suit you, you should not have any difficulty doing so, since it is indeed the one-and-only change that would bring you eternal bliss and unimaginable rewards. Besides, there are considerable worldly incentives that will come your way. It is a truly win-win thing for you. You win the grace of Allah, and you win a life of great amenities here for the rest of your days—

THE FRAUD

How so? I mean, the amenities business?

THE FASCIST

Patience, my friend. We will spell them out for you at an appropriate juncture.

THE FRAUD

I am beginning to regret having used that slang, "spell out." Ever since, you have become a spelling bee...

THE FASCIST

What is a "spelling bee?" I have heard of the honey bee, but never of a spelling bee. Is it a variety of bee?

THE FRAUD

Come on, man—don't be pain in the arse.

THE FASCIST

Never heard of that either. Heard of pain in the *ass*, not pain in the *arse*...

THE FRAUD

Please, let's move on. Ass, arse—they're the same, okay? What is this, an English tutorial, and I am a tutor for your?

THE FASCIST

> A tooter for me? You better not! If you have to toot, you must first leave the room and do it outside.

THE FRAUD

> No, no, tutoring and tooting are not the same, you vulgar nut. Let's get on with it. We have important business to conduct.

THE FASCIST

> Do not get pissed, as you say. Is it okay for you to ask us all kinds of questions but not okay for us to ask you for an occasional clarification? We have every intention of perfecting our English so that we can deliver our next address to the United Nations with greater eloquence in English. Speaking of that do-nothing tool of the self-appointed five bullies reminds us of its predecessor, the League of Nations. The United Nations by its incompetence and partiality makes us nostalgic for its dead predecessor.

> But, on the other hand, we members of the Organisation of the Islamic Conference—the OIC—have gained great power in the U.N., and we will use it to compel infidels worldwide not to criticize Allah, Islam or its Holy Text and Prophet. They must be forced to accept the Holy Sharia globally, because if you cannot criticize Islam, you cannot criticize Sharia law—it is that simple!

At this show of strength, suddenly the faux American leapt to his feet and became nauseatingly sycophantic, as if badly frightened. He shortly recovered himself to some extent, but it looked like his grip on reality was slowly but surely being eroded by the little tyrant.

THE FRAUD

> You don't need to perfect your English. It is already beyond perfect. I mean, using terms such as "nostalgic" and "predecessor." That's already heavy lifting. Please, let's move on.

THE FASCIST

> Heavy lifting? That is for porters, weight lifters and mechanical machines. And we are none of those. We shall hope that you explain that to us at a later time when you are in a better mood. We notice that you keep wiggling in your chair as if some ants have invaded your privates. Are you okay?

THE FRAUD

> Never mind. Just get on with it.

THE FASCIST

> As we were saying, it is critical that you embrace the true Islam so that we can pull our resources together to achieve our assignments—

THE FRAUD

> I've heard what you want, but you will have to give me a lot of good reasons to commit to such a thing, when I am already about as pro-Islam as it can get. And I've got other problems with my presidency that this will just exacerbate—

THE FASCIST

> Do not you go bellyaching, telling people about your problems. Half the people do not care, and the other half feel you deserve them, as the saying goes. You get three guesses: To which camp do we belong?

At that point, the vulgar nut doubled up with his blood-curdling laughter.

THE FRAUD

To a third camp.

THE FASCIST

Hunh—a third camp?

THE FRAUD

The creep camp.

And then he starts laughing his head off.

THE FASCIST

We are even. Now, get serious and tell me where you stand.

THE FRAUD

As you know, I was born to a Sunni family, and certain powerful Sunnis have always considered me one of their own. Throughout the years these people helped me financially— of course, through intermediaries, without leaving a trace. They helped get me admitted to Harvard Law School and paid my way for all those years. I feel a degree of indebtedness to them, so I play along, although not unwillingly.

I'm playing along as a Christian now—nothing wrong with that faith, either, and I like Baha'i too. I'm just really trying to get along with everybody because I'm actually quite skeptical, so I welcome nonbelievers as well. So, I can embrace Shi'ism too, like I did with the others, but, again, you will have to convince me why I should, as my Sunni friends and patrons will object quite loudly and violently, I imagine.

THE FASCIST

Yes, we are aware of your many heretical indiscretions. You will shed them all eventually. As for your current handlers, you will have many compelling reasons to come over to our camp instead. In that regard, feel free to raise any and as many questions you have, and, by the aid of Allah, we shall answer them for you.

THE FRAUD

Well, I've got an immediate problem that's probably related to your greasy proposal. And in deference to your wish that I leave the room when certain urges surge, I must do so right now. I have no idea what was in that delicious meal you had us served at lunch today. Not only is my mind spinning, but my system's in turmoil, and I must attend to it. Can we have a short break?

With that parting comment, the session recessed. I felt nauseated at the very thought of having the puppetmaster of the Free World's "leader" be any type of religious fanatic, regardless of the sect.

Act Seven

*W*ith hugs and kisses duly performed, the odd couple started their deliberation. By now they had staked out their turfs, to some degree. The Fascist acted like a representative of "On High," while the grease-pump Fraud assumed his transparently phony subservience role.

THE FASCIST

> As we mentioned earlier, it is vital that you take the two critical steps away from Sunni heresy and toward the Twelfth Imamate Shi'a true faith. Without so doing, there is little point in wasting our time by meeting *again*—

THE FRAUD

> I really don't think there is any need for an ultimatum. You promised to answer my questions, and I told you that I may enlist as a foot soldier of Sahib al-Zaman, the Lord of the Age, even though I'm not quite sure the whole thing isn't a bogus Shi'ite creation. What I am quite sure of is that you are clearly a delusional nutjob who is hallucinating reasons to be a megalomaniac.

> I admit, however, that you represent a power base of millions of people, whom you work very well, even though many million others detest

you. In my quest to get the whole world to like me, I'd like to learn your touch. For this reason, I can learn to overlook our many and vast differences, and focus on the common good—good for us too!

I learned much about Sunni Islam, I might as well become an adept at Shi'ism as well. Indeed, we have much in common, especially since we were both raised to love Islam, the Holy Prophet (saw) and Holy Quran. Your insight into the complexities of Shi'ism is useful. It's for this reason that I feel free to take advantage of this opportunity and present to you more thorny questions raised by Islam's detractors. Keep in mind that I'm raising these questions not solely for dispelling my *own* doubts but also for arming myself with the powerful explanations you supply to rebut the slanderous allegations of Islam's enemies. I'm playing devil's advocate, so to speak. I hope that you do clarify these questions, since you're indeed erudite in Islamic theology.

So far, I hadn't seen much of the Fraud's dark side— and many people believe he's just a great guy who doesn't have a dark side, but maybe he's just run by evil handlers. Anyway, I was willing to give him the benefit of the doubt, although many things I'd hear here were disturbing. I was almost feeling sympathetic and sorry for the guy, and I was anxious to hear his points in common with the Fascist.

THE FASCIST

We have no formal training in our sacred scripture. What we know comes from studying whenever we have a chance at the feet of our Point of Emulation—the Supreme Leader on Shi'a law, Ayatollah Mesbah Yazdi. He is a gem, the man is. We must also confess, in confidence, that we receive help from On High.

When our nerves are frayed by the unceasing machinations of the enemies and from the burden of our duties as the leader vessel for the Sahib al-Zaman, we partake of the most soothing and comforting medication. It is during these blissful states that we are informed of the reality of things and provided priceless insight and guidance.

THE FRAUD

Remarkable, indeed. Now I can see how any one man can be a repository of such seemingly infinite knowledge and wisdom. So, you really believe you're receiving direct help from On High? Was the "hidden imam" the apparition you've talked about seeing and receiving instruction from, as you stated at the U.N.? He is also the Twelfth Imam to the Shi'a, the *Mahdi* or Messiah, whom Sunnis also anticipate, right? You Shi'a believe that Sahib al-Zaman—the last of the Prophet's direct lineage—never died, but when five years old fell into a well, where he still lives, am I right? And that he will return any day now to bring about justice for the true believers of Allah?

THE FASCIST

Yes, that is correct—very good. As the elixir soothes my nerves, I am transported by luminous angels to a different realm. And it is during this transported state that all kinds of mysteries are revealed and further instructions on how I must conduct the affairs of the world are given to me. You see, in this way I am indeed the Chosen One—Allah has chosen me to receive His greatest dispensation.

THE FRAUD

This is priceless. I couldn't have asked for a better display of your megalomaniacal delusions and insane illusions—but they work very well for you, so long as your regime stays intact. To continue with the play—in which you act so well—people say that it is during your visits to the Jamkaran mosque near the city of Qom, where Sahib al-Zaman has been reportedly holed up in that well for over a thousand years, that you have gotten your insights and marching orders.

THE FASCIST

Yes, it is at that hallowed spot where we receive most of our guidance. We never visit his sanctified precinct without having prayed earnestly, taken a large dose of our soothing medication to empty ourself from ourself and open up fully to receive his missives. Yet, at times of great need, provided that we pray from the heart and take our medication, His Blessedness Imam Zaman Mahdi comes to our help anywhere that we may be.

THE FRAUD

Come on! You and I both know that tourist trap Jamkaran is a *bogus* shrine you expanded in order to give your regime a "sacred" site both to scam poor and unsuspecting pilgrims—and to serve as a means by which you can claim divine authority. Nice touch, tossing the scroll with Imam Zaman's name on it into the well there. Man, your priestly class has been working overtime with that hoax! How many millions has selling false dreams to the unwashed masses made the clergy so far?

And, do tell me—how can someone who can't work his way out of a well for over a thousand years suddenly come out and transform this world into a reflection of heaven? The idea that a child fearing for his life hides in a well and stays there for all these centuries sounds bogus and creepy. Again, at the risk of repeating myself, I'm raising these questions to arm myself with answers to the faithless people who make a mockery of Islam.

THE FASCIST

It sounds creepy only to the creeps—creatures of no faith. No false modesty is indicated here— the fact is that, over the years, I have been transformed by the Sahib al-Zaman from merely another blind-in-the-heart, run-of-the-mill mortal to his very personal emissary. How did this happen? I have witnessed his reality numberless times with the eye of faith. Again, I say all this to you in confidence since it is this kind of information that fuels the fire of the enemies.

THE FRAUD

I appreciate the confidence, I guess. How's this:

I sense the invisible hand of Sahib al-Zaman in arranging this opportunity for me. I am eager to sit at your feet for as long as it takes for you to clarify the issues raised against the faith and confirm my own conviction.

I was startled to hear the American-Internationalist use a perfect Persian accent in emulation of the diminutive freak. He really was a great actor, as many had suspected. I thought this all was just very fascinating— and the show did go on, with the Napoleon-complex fellow puffing out his chest as if the other's obsequious arrow had been true and had met its mark.

THE FASCIST

Nice—very nice! Certainly, you may do so.

THE FRAUD

> These issues I raise pop in my head randomly. I
> hope you don't mind. I am sure you can answer
> them as they come to me.

THE FASCIST

> Well, once again you are in need of your
> teleprompter to organize your thoughts. But, go
> ahead and ask. However, our nerves are
> extremely frayed right now. As you may have
> noticed, our hands tremor, and we are yawning
> uncontrollably. We need a short break to
> partake of our medication, after which we shall
> proceed with enunciating the answers you
> seek.

*Then the Fascist snapped his fingers, and the Thick
Thug appeared quicker than a genie would emerge after
his lantern is rubbed. "Our medication," he barked at
the Thick Thug, then turned to the Fraud.*

THE FASCIST

> Many years ago, our Point of Emulation noticed
> our troubled digestive system. In his infinite
> wisdom he prescribed an excellent remedy—

THE FRAUD

> Is Ayatollah Yazdi a doctor?

THE FASCIST

> Refrain yourself from interrupting us with
> irrelevant and disrespectful questions about
> our Point of Emulation, who is divinely
> ordained and inspired.

THE FRAUD

> Yeah, right. That claim doesn't surprise me,
> though. It seems everybody in this boys club is
> "divinely ordained"—when can I join? What a
> great gig, being all holy and everything. It's a

step up even from being the President of the U.S.

THE FASCIST

As we were saying, the Ayatollah, himself a victim of digestive complications, had discovered the cure and shared with us his medicine. It is a true elixir. Not only does it settle my digestive discomfort, it envelopes me with calmness and transports me to a state of complete bliss. You shall see for yourself as soon as our laggard attendant hurries up and brings it to us.

Act Eight

*B*efore a minute's lapse, the Thick Thug returned to the room with a tray full of the Fascist's medication and its paraphernalia. The tray contained "manghal va vaafoor"—a charcoal burner and pipe—with several pencil-size sticks of his "medicine": opium.

In no time, the greasy sleaze sliced a piece of the opium, placed it on the orifice of the special "hugheh" or pipe, and, using tongs, raised a glowing red charcoal to the opium. The heat of the charcoal gently burned the opium, and the dictator dragged hungrily on the pipe.

Okay folks, now you know what the Fascist has been smoking, when he launches on his idiotic public rants. He can't be blamed: He is indeed receiving inspiration, not from "On High," as he claims, but from the "high" of his medication!

The Fraud, not exactly a stranger to smoking himself, sat transfixed and became a second-hand smoker, since the sizzling opium fume rapidly saturated the air in the cage-like room. Suddenly, I understood why the small room was chosen: It is the kind of space ideally suited for smoking opium. The tiny, windowless room traps the heavy opium smoke, and the parties present get to breathe it in and get the maximum bang for their buck, so to speak. Having taken several deep drags, the despot turned the pipe to the phony, who was warming up to the whole experience.

THE FRAUD

> Thank you, bro. Although I've done a lot of "medications" in the past, I presently limit myself to an occasional cigarette and some wine. The sanctimonious public is on my back for even smoking tobacco. Unlike Slick Willy— who was forced to admit that he had smoked marijuana but tried to cover his arse by saying that, while he *did* smoke it, he did not *inhale* it—I am honest enough to confess that I *have* inhaled and I *do* inhale.

With that, he lit up a cigarette and took a big drag.

THE FASCIST

> Two things: Tobacco is harmful. It causes cancer. And as for your taking wine on occasions, that is a clear violation of the sacred ordinances of the Islamic faith, unless you do so properly—

THE FRAUD

> *Mea culpa*—guilty as charged. But again, you and I both know that many Muslims imbibe the "Satanic Brew"—alcohol—prohibited or not. It is just human. We humans are not angels, and we need things like that to calm our nerves.

THE FASCIST

> Yes, there are Muslims who do imbibe the satanic brew. Why do that if you can calm your nerves by what is not forbidden, like what I am doing now? If you have to imbibe, then, as I said, there is a proper way of so doing—

THE FRAUD

> Well, there are those who find the satanic brew more appealing than what you are smoking. As you know and are basically admitting, many high-ranking Shi'ite clerics *do* drink alcohol

often, but I understand that they rinse their mouths before prayers. Is that what you mean by saying that there is a proper way of drinking booze?

THE FASCIST

Yes, you pre-empted what we wanted to say. Where do you get your information about our high clerics imbibing the satanic brew?

THE FRAUD

The usual source: Our CIA people tell us that the Iraqi Kurds do a brisk business transporting all kinds of booze across the border to Iran. The agents asked the Kurds if they weren't running the risk of the clerics having them arrested and hanged. Do you want to know what the mule Kurds who ferried the brew said?

THE FASCIST

We can only guess. It seems American spies are busier than ever, despite all our saber-rattling and show of strength. I would say you too are a spy, but I know that you are sufficiently Islamized and coercible that I do not fear your treachery. You have repeatedly demonstrated your acceptance of Islam as a great religion, and this much makes us brothers in faith to whatever extent, although there is room for improvement, about which I hope to convince you during your visit here.

So, to let you in on a secret, yes, we also regularly avail ourself of the satanic brew. In fact, we have a supply of Shiraz wine here. Never travel very far without it. It is the color of tea, and no one can tell the difference from afar. The difference is indeed there. We will have it served with our next...

The Fascist did not complete the sentence as he drifted into a deep, trance-like state. He was so "calm" that he could barely speak. He only nodded from time to time, and his head tilted sideways with drops of saliva further staining his already filthy collar. The small, windowless room was enveloped by a thick cloud of opium smoke, and the second-hand-smoker—willingly or not—kept breathing in what the opiate aficionados call "heavenly aroma," at which point he also began to appear drowsy. Yet, he went on, once the other man began to speak.

THE FRAUD

> Well, the Kurd mules said that there was no such risk at all, because the high clerics across the border are their best customers. "Why would they want to punish *us*," they said, "the very people who carry heavy cases of the alcohol on our backs through the treacherous terrain to supply them with what they desperately want? They are our best protectors against the border people who want a cut of the stuff for themselves." Needless to say, it is extremely hypocritical for you and the rest of your thug ayatollahs, imams and mullahs to be boozing while pretending to be devout Muslims and forcing the common people upon whom you prey to go without.

Unperturbed by anything his "brother"-cum-competitor could possibly bring up at this point, before long the Fascist drifted into a deep sleep. The Thick Thug brought a pillow, gently placed it under his tilting head, and took away the tray of medication. The Fraud, having done a great deal of second-hand smoking, fared only a little better. Noticing his cellmate being almost comatose, he leaned back, and in no time the two played a sickening, out-of-phase duet that sounded strangely like the snoring of two Iowa hogs, an idea that would no doubt have upset these would-be brothers in a faith that abhorred all things porcine.

Act Nine

*T*he Fraud was first to stir awake, although he still showed signs of opium intoxication. He kept yawning, scratching his behind and picking his nose with great diligence. Having gotten those tasks out of the way, he gently nudged the still comatose Fascist in the ribcage, hoping to wake him up. All he got was a grunt that interrupted the creep's rhythmic snoring. The taller man, not one to give up easily, kicked the megalomaniac harder, this time on the little worm's backside. Sure enough, it did some good, and the Fascist opened his eyes partially, to show his opium-stained teeth.

Then the door opened, and the Thick Thug appeared with a tray full of treats: Freshly brewed tea, delicate Persian pastries, mixed nuts, shelled pistachio nuts and a huge platter full of the very best fruit that Afghanistan could produce. For a change, The Fraud opened the session, his exotic intoxication releasing his inhibitions and inspiring him to play to the hilt the new part he was being offered.

THE FRAUD

> Wow, this looks like a sample of the promised Paradise—all these magnificent delicacies. If only instead of your attendant, a dozen virgins were serving us, I'd think that I'd been transported to Allah's lush Paradise, praised be His blessed name. Now, that's what I'm talking

about—I'm starting to attain to the devout Shi'ite mind.

THE FASCIST

This is nothing, what you see on this mundane earth. Having taken our medication, we were indeed transported into the realm of true ecstasy. How we deeply yearn to remain in that state of indescribably precious euphoria, free from all worldly concerns, and immersed in joy. Alas, that is not to be. We have our work to do. Yet, that time is coming. And what we experience in this state of transport is only a glimpse of what awaits us in Allah's Paradise. Yes, we will have the best food, drinks, lush fruits and the virgins as well, both wide-eyed *houris* and young boys with pearl earrings, to fulfill our every need. And I do mean *every* need.

THE FRAUD

Well, I'll pass on the man-boy stuff. But tell me, will the boys with the pearl earrings naturally have mascara around their eyes, like the coming messiah the Mahdi?

Anyway, it's 72 *female* virgins to every devout man, right? That is one point that confuses me about Islam—what detractors always point to, and I have to admit, they've got a point. Critics and nonbelievers also point to the whole religious brainwashing here: Deprive your victims—er—*subjects* of all this stuff now so they will do all sorts of crazy and violent sh— to get it later. That way, all who are getting it now don't have to share with the foot soldiers for Allah. If I may be cynical—and it's clear you are rubbing off on me—it's quite a brilliant plot.

Not sure I like all this stuff, but I've got to spend a great deal of time justifying and apologizing for Islam. I just ignore the pesky details and call Islam a "great religion" and a "religion of peace," even though practically its entire history has been full of violent conquest, costing the lives of some 270 million people worldwide.

Now that I am in this altered state of truth-speaking, I feel so phony and fraudulent saying all that apologist blarney, when I know about all the gnarly parts of Islamic doctrine and history.

And then there's this eternal virginity bit in Paradise—I mean, who has that kind of stamina?

THE FASCIST

Look, would the all-merciful Allah bestow upon you that kind of blessing and not include in the package deal the necessary means you need to enjoy the gift? Thinking such thoughts is tantamount to blasphemy. Banish them.

Have you not read the debates between the religious scholars on this subject? They are very concerned with whether or not we true believers will receive a perpetual erection in Paradise—the Egyptian religious scholar Al-Suyuti says we will, and we believe him! You do your job, and Allah will see to it that you get your rewards—the full complement.

THE FRAUD

Then tell me, just so I can answer critics who wonder the same thing: Do these virgins *stay* virgins? I mean, after they are deflowered? Do the men get to start all over again, every time?

Another question about this virgin thing came up one time when my *manzel* and I were discussing this very topic. She was so pissed off. She screamed at me, "We get screwed in *this* world by you worthless men, and we have to look forward to being whores by the dozens in the afterlife too?"

As you know, my *manzel* is somewhat of a Christian. It is really a requirement in America to have some kind of religious affiliation, preferably Christian of some kind. You can't get very far in office otherwise, so that explains my outward faith.

THE FASCIST

First of all, as concerns your vulgar question regarding the virgins, that too is a matter of debate among our scholars. However, it is my opinion that they must remain virgins—after all, to a true Muslim, virginity is the highest prized quality of a female, and her worth goes down markedly after she has been sullied by another man.

Secondly, we note that you and your *manzel* have in common your hatred of America. We have read her poorly written thesis from Princeton, in which she expresses her hatred of America because it is a white racist society.

In our thick file we have records of things you have publicly said and done that also indicate you share that hatred with her, as well as having additional hatred for the fact that the United States is run by Zionists and is the deadly enemy of our faith.

From your comments, you would fit in well in our administration, but the Iranian people may not like you, because deep in their hearts they love America and Americans. You read the papers. All the reports about how Iranians hospitably treat any American tourist they meet, how our young emulate your culture, dance to your music and lap up everything with the least American flavor to it? This satanic corruption of our great Islamic Republic is very infuriating and another thing we will need your help to end. Unfortunately, we cannot kill these America-loving traitors fast enough—there are so many millions of them. How could they choose America over Allah's Holy Islamic Republic of Iran? It must be the satanic American CIA behind it all.

But we have proof of your hatred for America, which is why you will help me. There is one piece of evidence that I particularly liked, so I brought it along. Let me share it with you, so that we both can really enjoy it.

THE FRAUD

I'm sure you've got nothing, but go ahead. Oh, and by the way, I know the Persian people love America—that is why the West has not destroyed your country. There are millions of good human beings in your country, but they want to be free of *you*—when they escape from Iran, they drop Shi'ism like a hot potato—so I still can't imagine why I would want to help you.

THE FASCIST

Just more filthy satanic infidels who will roast in hell—Allahu akbar! Now, let me see—oh, here it is. It is the piece from the American TV show "Meet the Press" that aired on Sunday, September 7, 2008. You were a senator at the time. You were asked about your stance on the American Flag by General Bill Ginn USAF (Ret.) to explain why you do not follow protocol when the National Anthem is played. The general stated to you that according to the United States Code, Title 36, Chapter 10, Sec. 171, during rendition of the national anthem, when the flag is displayed, all present (except those in uniform) are expected to stand at attention facing the flag with the right hand over the heart. Or, at the very least, stand and face it. Remember that?

Now, this is the best part. You came right out and stated:

"As I've said about the flag pin, I don't want to be perceived as taking sides. There are a lot of people in the world to whom the American flag is a symbol of oppression... The anthem itself conveys a war-like message. You know, the bombs bursting in air and all that sort of thing."

You really topped that by saying:

"The National Anthem should be 'swapped' for something less parochial and less bellicose. I like the song 'I'd Like to Teach the World to Sing.' If that were our anthem, then, I might salute it. In my opinion, we should consider reinventing our National Anthem as well as redesigning our Flag to better offer our enemies hope and love."

Wow, this really delighted me. But you didn't stop there. You went on:

"It's my intention, if elected, to disarm America to the level of acceptance to our Middle East Brethren. If we, as a Nation of warring people, conduct ourselves like the nations of Islam, where peace prevails...perhaps a state or period of mutual accord could exist between our governments. When I become President, I will seek a pact of agreement to end hostilities between those who have been at war or are in a state of enmity, and institute a freedom from disquieting oppressive thoughts. We, as a Nation, have placed upon the nations of Islam an injustice, which is why my wife disrespects the Flag, and she and I have attended several flag-burning ceremonies in the past."

Honesty on your part? A rare practice, huh? Were you under the influence, by any chance?

Then you went on, "Of course now, I have found myself about to become the President of the United States, and I have put my hatred aside." Now, I have to give it to you. That was very clever to cover your exposed behind. Finally, you concluded, "I will use my power to bring change to this Nation and offer the people a new path." By the way, did you hear our applause all the way from Iran as we watched the clip of your exquisite performance?

After he finished his diatribe impugning the Fraud as being rabidly anti-American, I was curious how the latter would respond. From his ashen color and the furious look on his face, I guessed he was very angry. Although he seem slightly charmed previously, his eyes narrowed, and he suddenly became hostile.

THE FRAUD

Save the applause, send money, as the saying goes. First of all, you depraved idiot, that "Meet the Press" story is totally bogus, a complete hoax—it never happened, and I never said any of that. You never saw such a thing with your own eyes, you lying sack of crap. You probably made up the whole rumor yourself—that's the kind of trash you engage in. You'll say and do anything for your "cause," won't you? You're an egomaniac, and you just can't let me into your little clique, can you? But you know I've won, so that's why I'm here.

And you would be completely wrong about my wife and me hating America. But we *are* citizens of the world, which means we can get along with just about anybody, even the likes of you.

Now, if it's not too much to ask, settle this virgin thing for me, will you? What do the virgins get for servicing the men? Only sex maniacs like you and your crew? Or do the women go next door and get 72 young studs each to service *them* in compensation? I mean, in Allah's justice women would want their fair shake, or don't they count?

THE FASCIST

The only "shake" women receive is what they get *before* going to what you called next door and a possible 72 studs...

The wretched little pervert winked at the other man, as if his sexual renown had preceded him.

THE FRAUD

Look, I'm not finished. Hear me out. When we have arguments like that, you know what she does? She wouldn't let me have any for a whole week. She calls it a "time out." Just like in sports, time out from action. Crap she learned reading some psychology trash. It's a form of punishment for misbehavior, recommended to keep children in line. What they do is take privileges away from the child for a certain duration. For instance, they don't let the child watch her favorite television program for a week. And she uses that on me. Not only wouldn't she let me have what I am entitled to as her husband, but she also wouldn't let me sleep in our bed, so I have to curl up on a damned couch, which, in the White House, isn't so bad after all.

But the whole thing seems un-Islamic to me, brother. Sometimes when I think about it, I do like how the Ummah keeps its women in line—

nobody to give you guff, no matter how many you have. The Prophet Muhammad (pbuh), while he himself had many wives, limited his followers to four. But, as you say, under Shi'a one can have as many *sigheh* or "temporary wives" as one wishes—it sounds more appealing all the time.

Hearing the Fraud join the sexist and misogynistic side of things struck me as very worrisome, and I felt sickened by it. I hoped it wasn't a foreshadowing of him absorbing other bad influences from the vile woman-oppressor and murderer sitting in front of him. I hoped it was just because he was stoned and drunk—from substances frequently used in brainwashing, as exemplified Islamically by the cult of the Hashshashin, the assassins who brainwashed young men to behave violently by getting them intoxicated and showing them a glimpse of the "heavenly fruits of Paradise" in an earthly *garden specially created for the purpose. From all the contradiction, I was beginning to see in the American, I was afraid I was watching just such a process in action, before my very eyes.*

THE FASCIST

Now, you look here—that is why Rasul Allah specifically stipulated in the Holy Quran that women must be subservient to men, and if they misbehave they should be punished corporally— we beat women, stone them, hang them, cover them up. Whatever it takes.

Remember, according to Sharia law, a woman is worth only half as much as a man, a man can beat his wife and kill her if she dishonors him or his family. The Holy Sharia allows us to completely dominate, exploit, enslave and oppress women as much as we want and is possible.

Do you or do you not see the wisdom of his ordinances? Women are like animals. They have a function to perform and must be kept in line. You have to crack the whip whenever they misbehave, which can be often enough, to put them back in their cages. That is what happens when the *kafir* world begins to give in to all this crap about gender equality and violates the provisions of the Holy Quran.

THE FRAUD

Yeah, I can see that. Let me tell you when she goes into that equality-uppity mode—which is often enough—and keeps me away, I end up doubling and even tripling my smoking. I understand this is a form of sublimation—channeling the erotic urge into a different form of activity that's supposed to be pleasurable. I don't think smoking and you-know-what are equally pleasurable, not by a long shot. But that's what I do. Oh yeah, and I do take a few more drinks than usual, I must confess—

THE FASCIST

Allow us to tell you an illustrative story about one of our Muslim brethren, as an example of how *we* deal with women. A very shy guy, he was, so he goes to his village mullah to get help. After fidgeting for a long time and the mullah encouraging him to speak up, he apologizes profusely and says, "May I be forgiven if I ask a very personal question?" The mullah, being an understanding and helpful guy who is willing to assist any and all, says, "Sure, my son. That is why I am here."

The man fidgets some more, and, after more urging by the mullah, he says, "Again, I apologize for asking this personal question. How do you indicate to your *manzel* you want her to visit you in your bed? I mean, I am really embarrassed to come right out and ask my *manzel*." The mullah says, "I whistle, and she knows that I am in the mood, and *she* comes to *me*."

The fellow is impressed yet looks puzzled. After fidgeting some more he says, "You have four wives—when you whistle, how would they know which one you are summoning?"

The mullah smiles from ear-to-ear and replies, "I have a different tune for each wife." The brother, still puzzled, says he has a follow-up question, and the mullah tells him to ask it.

The man then remarks, "That is excellent, the way you have a different tune for each wife. Pray tell me, what if a wife has the desire to join you in bed? How is it communicated to your person?"

The mullah shoots back, "It is very simple, my son. She comes to me and asks, 'Your person, did you whistle?'"

The Fascist howled at length enjoying his own storytelling, revealing his rust-colored teeth, before the Fraud then took over.

THE FRAUD

I thought I knew a lot about you. But I didn't know you're also a sex maniac and obsessed with matters related to sex. Can we move on?

THE FASCIST

It is the medication—the stuff puts us into this mood. But, a sex maniac we are not. We are only a red-blooded healthy male who finds the activity most enjoyable. Is that not the reason that Rasul Allah has allowed us men numerous wives?

Do you not know that women are simply *awrah*, walking vaginas? In Islam, every part that a woman is not allowed to show is her *awrah*, and in the true faith of Shi'a, that means all parts except for her face and hands. As it says in the great hadith by Waliuddin Abu Abdullah Mahmud Tabrizi: "A woman is like a private part. When she goes out, the devil casts a glance at her."

Do you not recall that the Holy Quran says a woman is worth only one-half as much as a man? Have you not read in the Quran, "Women are your fields: go, then, into your fields whence you please?"

The sacred text also says we men are in charge and can beat our property if she gets out of line. And this is the way Allah ordained it. Men can do no wrong, and everything is to be blamed on the woman. This is why we beat, stone or hang women for being raped—they have caused the man to behave badly, as he sullies another man's property. Therefore, she has wronged two men directly—and many others indirectly, including all her male relatives. She has sullied the family honor, and she must pay for it.

These are some of the Islamic teachings on women, who are inferior to us and unclean. You cannot be a selective Muslim: When provisions and laws suit you, you go by them, but you ignore the ones you do not like. No! Being a Muslim is a package deal. You either take all of the Quran and live by it, or you do not.

THE FRAUD

Let's drop this subject of Islamic sexism and misogyny, as it makes me uncomfortable about being a believer. Allow me to continue asking you other questions. Although you are not a mullah, you are just like the one in your story, willing to entertain my questions, and you have told me I can and should ask anything that comes to me. Remember that hollow reed thing you said before? I believe that.

You see, my wife and I argue a lot. Psychologists say different professions attract people with proclivity to those professions. I believe that. Lawyers, for instance, are your more-than-average-quibbling-and-argumentative type. That's the reason, in part, that they gravitate to law. Those with violent temperaments tend to go to police work or the military. And so on.

During one of our many arguments, my wife started attacking Islam and marshaled her legal mind to try to rattle my faith with logic. Believe me, she is smart. A lot smarter than I am—

THE FASCIST

I buy that, just about anybody is.

THE FRAUD

Okay Jack, would you let me finish?

THE FASCIST

Jack?

THE FRAUD

Yeah, short for jackass, a rude and dumb jackass. That's what you are.

THE FASCIST

Thank you, Mr. Decorum-Genius. Go ahead and finish.

THE FRAUD

Well, this time she was objecting to my public statements about Islam. She said, "You keep going around and endlessly parroting the same absurd line about Islam, *ad infinitum.*" She likes to use the little Latin expressions she knows all the time. And she went on saying:

"You stand in public and say Islam is the religion of peace. How could you say that with a straight face and so shamelessly when actually you know many Muslims are hotheads who commit violence based on so many passages in the Quran? In fact, you know full well that there are numerous passages that have incited believers to violence, like Dutch politician Geert Wilders showed in his movie 'Fitna.' Here is just one such scripture or *ayah*: 'When the sacred months have passed away, then slay the idolaters wherever you find them, and take them captives and besiege them and lie in wait for them in every ambush.'"

She really makes a big deal about those verses, even though I tell her they are taken out of context. She shouts, "Don't bullsh— me! It's the fanatics *themselves* who take them out of context as a pretext for murdering all non-Muslims!"

Then she concludes, "The Bible says, 'By their fruit shall ye know them.' And in the house of Muhammad, I see only fruitcakes." She meant *crazies*. How do you like that?

THE FASCIST

I do not. But she is right about our scriptures: In order to throw the stupid infidels off our scent, we pretend that these verses are "taken out of context" when it suits us. Otherwise, we ourselves take them "out of context" and use them to kill infidels—it is that simple... But, are you finished?

I could see that the sadistic jerk was enjoying his violent comment, as he grinned broadly.

THE FRAUD

No, no, I'm just warming up. Bear with me, and let me go on. She continued:

"I keep looking to find the peaceful Islam you and the rest trumpet about, and all I find is a bunch of feuding, intolerant killers. Where the hell is the peaceful Islam? Would the peaceful Islam please stand up so we all can see it? The house Muhammad built is crammed with numberless sects, sub-sects, schools and so on. Each and every one of them pronounces every other one as *kuffar* or apostates. Not only do they war with non-Muslims, they also go murdering each other in the most barbaric ways known to man. They bomb each other's marketplaces, funeral processions and even mosques. As a trained lawyer you need to go with the facts on the ground rather than have your head in your ditty bag."

Do you know what a "ditty bag" is?

THE FASCIST

No, I do not.

THE FRAUD

Among other things, "ditty bag" means "arse" in British slang.

THE FASCIST

Give her credit, then, for I have noticed that myself. You do, frequently enough, have your head in your ditty bag.

And he lets out one of his nauseating laughs while the Fraud squirmed and fluttered like a wounded rooster.

THE FRAUD

Why don't you pay me for making you laugh? I'll try to dignify it by calling what you emit—

the *donkey-braying*, that is—a "laugh." So, what would you say to her?

THE FASCIST

Silence.

THE FRAUD

"Silence?" What kind of rebuttal is that?

THE FASCIST

It was Satan who was speaking through her to shake your faith. In instances like this one, the more you try to respond, the more your faith will be undermined. You cannot win against the accursed Satan. I have it from Rasul Allah's rightful heir, Imam Ali himself: In response to a Satan-manipulated fool's question, the Imam said in Farsi, *Javabe ablahaan khamosheest*— "the appropriate response to a fool is silence."

THE FRAUD

Hey, that's cute, but it wouldn't wash in the present world. No court of law I know of would accept that argument. But tell me, did Imam Ali speak Farsi?

THE FASCIST

Yes, indeed he did—only *one* of his least important attributes and abilities. And some moron Iranians, just because the gem is in Farsi, claim that it is not his.

THE FRAUD

My impression was that Ali was a big killer with his fearsome sword that had its own name. What was it? Let me think...

THE FASCIST

"Zolfaghar" was the name of his mighty sword, which Allah imbued with magical powers. With this blessed weapon brought to earth by Adam out of the Garden of Eden, Imam Ali slaughtered many infidels.

THE FRAUD

That's really impressive. And people said that the man was illiterate, just like his cousin and father-in-law, Muhammad (pbuh). Well, just about everyone was illiterate in those days in that part of the world. That's nothing to be ashamed of.

THE FASCIST

Not only was Imam Ali *not* illiterate, he was in regular communication with On High, and he received a great number of missives and shared them with his devotees. Among the treasures he bestowed upon humanity is a collection of his priceless "brief sayings" called *kalemaate-al-Ghesaar*, which encapsulated mankind's best—

THE FRAUD

Now that you mention it, I heard about that. I also heard people say that some of Ali's sycophants really put that book together and then merely attributed it to him. The infidel scholars also say that the Holy Quran itself is just a patchwork of older texts and that Muhammad (pbuh) did not receive it from On High, but that it was composed much later, after he left this earth. In fact, some of them are now claiming that Muhammad did not even exist!

THE FASCIST

Look, Imam Ali was not the run-of-the-mill human being. As a matter of fact, some of his adoring people go to the extreme by venerating him. These people are known as *Ali-al-allahi.*

They claim that Ali is not Allah, yet he is not apart from Allah. Their adoration of the Imam carries them a bit too far. We Twelvers—devotees of the Twelfth Imam—pay him the homage he rightfully deserves, but we do not go as far as *Ali-al-allahi* do.

As concerns the vicious and filthy lies you have just recounted about Rasul Allah and the Holy Quran, we can only say that we know some of our brethren or even some Sunni infidels will soon behead all those who insult Islam in this manner.

THE FRAUD

Unfortunately, the world has become quite used to the hotheaded behavior of Muslims, although I personally am working hard to distract everyone away from the issue of Islamic terrorism by not using that very phrase to describe it.

Anyway, we got sidetracked again, but it was worth it to me. And since we are sidetracked, let me ask you something on a different subject. May I?

THE FASCIST

Sure, go ahead.

THE FRAUD

I'm just curious—so you have your doctorate in traffic engineering. I know that you spent some time with the Revolutionary Guard. Some claim you served as their executioner and personally put bullets into the heads of many political prisoners. You got your stripes by your murderous services, they say. Then you got rewarded and made the mayor of Tehran. And now you are the President of the Islamic Republic. But, tell me, when you worked as professor of traffic engineering, did you teach the cops the various methods of extortion— shaking down motorists to ante-up some cash?

At this point, the Fraud doubled up with laughter, enjoying his jab at the Fascist. You could tell the lingering effect of opium was making him sillier than he usually is. He kept giggling between his roars of laughter. As for the sleazy murderer, he maintained a poker face during the prolonged, one-sided hilarity, before counter-punching.

As I sat watching from the safe distance of my adopted home of America—for whose freedoms I was immensely grateful—hearing the name "Tehran" made me very sad and homesick for the beautiful land of my youth. I wanted so badly for Iran to be free so I could leisurely stroll its lovely streets in the open, rather than sneaking around like I had briefly done to get these tapes. With the look of how things were developing between these two world leaders, I was beginning to fear that liberation would never happen, despite the fervent wishes of millions of Iranians both at home and abroad.

THE FASCIST

What use is it if you get trained but do not make use of your training? Did you not use your Harvard legal education to train ACORN crooks in how to cheat the government and how to stuff ballot boxes to get you elected President? And we both know how stuffing boxes has been critical to getting us elected, so we could eventually meet as the heads of our respective states.

Speaking of elections, people have the naïve notion that elections should be honest, governments should be honest, businesses should be honest, people should be honest, and on and on and on. What an absurd expectation! There is no such thing as an honest election to begin with. "Your" country,

America, is not a democracy. It is a plutocracy, the rule of money and the moneyed people. And that is where the Jews come in. In our country, we have this title of "republic," implying that the public rules. Nothing could be further from reality. See, I did not use the word "truth," abiding by your request. As for us, we have a theocracy with an absolute ruler in the person of the Supreme Jurist.

And speaking of people and governments, here is a stark reality: People do all they can to cheat the government and the government cheats all the people. It is a cheat world, is it not?

THE FRAUD

Man, you floor me every time you speak. What can I say?

THE FASCIST

What you can say is to embrace the call of the Sahib al-Zaman and say, "I believe in him" and recite the full Shahada—our Islamic creed: "There is no Allah, but Allah, Muhammad his Messenger (pbuh), and Ali his Guardian." Then we can continue our deliberations.

THE FRAUD

I recall reciting the Shahada as a boy, so I don't need to do it again, but I see you Shi'ites have added the little part at the end about Ali being Allah's "Guardian." I can see how the Sunnis would be annoyed with you—heck, they hate your Shi'ite guts—for basically taking over their religion. The Arabs are, after all, the true people of Muhammad (pbuh), while the Iranians are not. In fact, Arab raiders invaded Persia and took it over, destroying the old Persian culture and forcing the inhabitants to become Muslim at the point of that very famous Islamic sword. Even with your stories about Ali's magical sword and al-Zaman in the well, some say that Iranians are only slaves to the Arabs, that you have no culture of your own....

In any case, it's getting late, and we had a hard day. What you are asking me to do would be the hardest acting job of my life—and my Sunni friends would have a cow if I did that. Have a cow—do you know what means? It means they'll get royally pissed off. Anyway, I really need a little time to think it over and make sure when I make the commitment it will be from the heart and with all my being. Can we take up this issue first thing in the morning?

A nod of the head by the Fascist brought the session to an end.

Act Ten

*W*hen the tape resumed, the self-adoring, imitation human being, deeply impressed by his use of English idioms, intoned, *"No time to beat around the bush. Let's get down to brass tacks."* He was swiftly answered by the other phony.

THE FRAUD

Sure, sure. Earlier you advised *me* about being patient, but I see that you are not practicing what you preach. Be a bit patient with me. As I said at the end of our last meeting, this is the most difficult decision of my life, and I need to give it due consideration—

THE FASCIST

Well, have you? Let us get on with it.

THE FRAUD

Being the practical man that I am, I want you to tell me what's in it for me to "convert," because my Sunni friends would say I'm falling for the ridiculous lies of you and your priesthood, pretending like some delusional nutcase that you are receiving instructions essentially from Allah Himself. So, give me my motivation and explain what you alluded to earlier—about it being a great thing for me here in *this* world as well as in the afterlife. Well, the afterlife still remains to be seen, much as I would like believe in it. And as for benefits in *this* world, I basically have as much or more than any man could ever aspire to. I'm the President of the most powerful country in the world. Numberless people, including world leaders, kiss up to *me*—a black man—for a change; women swoon over me by the droves; and I can go on and on enumerating the long list of the perks I have.

You mentioned "amenities." What do you mean by that? Please explain, so I can make up my mind.

THE FASCIST

You keep throwing me curve balls, as you people like to say. First, you brag to me about having a long pri—?

THE FRAUD

No, no, no. You misheard me. I said "perks" not "pri—." A long list of *perks*, I said. Now who has a dirty mind?

THE FASCIST

Then tell me what "perks" means. You know that we are dead serious about mastering English, even English slang and colloquial English. All of it, so that we can be a good jihadist and help the Ummah establish Arabic as the only acceptable language in the world. As for the lies about being a puppet of the Arabs and His Blessedness being a fairytale, we should kill anyone who disrespects the Holy Faith like that. You are lucky, because you have a chance to redeem yourself by converting and becoming a disciple of the Supreme Leader.

THE FRAUD

> If you are not an Arab lap dog, as others say,
> then why are you stumping for Arabic to be the
> only acceptable language on earth? Why not
> the Farsi of your homeland?

THE FASCIST

> Arabic is the language of the Holy Quran, the
> divine revelation of Allah. It is the holy
> language. We pledge our allegiance to Islam,
> above and beyond all nations. I am first and
> foremost an Ummahist.

> The only reason you have not been killed before
> is because so many in the Ummah believe you
> are secretly one of us, as do many of "your"
> own people. But all you need to do, really, is
> give up the Sunni heresy and come over to us.

> Remember, two things tell us you are a
> Muslim: 1. Your father was a Muslim, albeit it
> a heretic, but much better than if only your
> mother had been a Muslima—which, of course,
> she was not; and 2. Your middle name Hussein
> is that of one of our most revered saints.

> You were warned years ago that you should not
> come here—do you honestly believe you can go
> now? You may have believed you could charm
> me! No, you are a fly in my spider web, so you
> have no choice. If you do not convert, we will
> not let you leave. And if you do convert, but if
> you are not sincere, you will have a very big
> bounty on your head for the rest of your life—
> nay, for eternity, *insha'Allah.* You know very
> well that such treachery as apostasy is
> punishable by death under our legal system.

THE FRAUD

> You can be sure that I regret having come here,
> although I have to admit some of my visit has

been pleasant. But I knew you would try to extort and blackmail me, and here you are. You can't be serious that you think you can prevent me from leaving. Even you can't be so megalomaniacal as to believe you could get away with such an absurd plan—but perhaps you *are* that insane.

But as long as I am here, I want you to elucidate all kinds of things for me, and I should be prepared to explain things you want to know. Fair enough. "Perks" is short for "perquisites," which means "privileges, benefits, advantages."

THE FASCIST

Am I supposed to turn green with envy? Do not let who you are now and what you have at present blind you to reality. As your friend, we will take time and spell things out for you. By the way, I really dig that spelling thing. I thank you for it.

Then he burst out with his trademark roaring hyena laughter. He seemed to relish using the word "dig." I just can't fathom why the creep found the word "dig" so hilarious. Who can figure out what goes on in that cranium of his?

THE FRAUD

I've been taught that something is funny when both parties laugh. So what's so funny, my helpful friend?

THE FASCIST

You really do not want to know, because it would upset you to no end.

THE FRAUD

Okay, finish laughing and get this show on the road. It's wearing my patience thin.

THE FASCIST

> Well, back to serious talk. You will love the amenities and "perks" we will be offering you. There are, however, two non-negotiable conditions. The first condition is that you convert to the true Islam—the Twelve Imamate Shi'a. And the second condition is that you call the Zionist dogs off our back and let us move forward—

THE FRAUD

> I dig your first condition, and I am almost there. What you need to spell out in greater detail is your second condition. I can't just give you carte blanche. Besides, if I make a commitment, I intend to keep it, but I might not be able to do so.

The smarmy dictator cracked a sly smile, as if he were relishing a moment of conquest.

THE FASCIST

> Am I the type who would do something like that to a friend? Would I ask you to do something that would get you in trouble or force you to go back on your promise?

THE FRAUD

> Frankly, the thought never crossed my mind—

THE FASCIST

> Stop right there and recant, Pinocchio. The long nose you have is stretching so far out that it is almost completely preventing us from seeing the other half of your face, not that it is worth seeing, anyway.

Hyena laughter again filled the little cage of the two beasts. The creep seemed to enjoy his own sense of humor. Then, with a snap of the fingers the Thick Thug appeared, at which point the Fascist commanded, "Bring us file 609 forthwith!"

With a thick file in hand, the Fascist began paging through it, keeping the Fraud in a deathly suspense for what seemed like a lifetime. As beads of sweat covered the American's face, he seemed to have difficulty breathing, and made a wheezing sound common in asthmatics.

THE FASCIST

> Sorry for bursting your balloon. You compelled us to do so by bragging about your position and the perks you have. You seem so intoxicated with the immediate and oblivious to the long-term. And not very long-term at that—

THE FRAUD

> Would you stop lecturing me and get to the specifics? I said a minute ago that my patience is wearing thin. By now, it's just about to disappear completely.

THE FASCIST

> You are most fortunate if you keep your position and perks until the next presidential election. We, for one, would not want to bet on that more than five of your worthless dollars. That is all—five "bucks," is it not?—and not a nickel more.

Even though they were supposed to be "brothers in faith," they could not resist the macho-male competition. After all, each wanted to top the other and be president of the whole world under the Ummah or community of believers that would soon attain global domination. I could tell that a big part of their blustering was an expression of admiration for each other's misdeeds and cons against the dirty infidels and unsuspecting voters.

THE FRAUD

Okay, Mr. Big Shot. Back that up. What makes you so sure? Do you have a crystal ball, or is it another one of those private inside revelations you get from what you call "On High?"

THE FASCIST

No, neither—just plain and simple earthly assessment of facts on the ground. And here they are. You are a fraud and a fake. It is all here in this file. Written records, pictures, testimonials by the most credible people that show beyond the slightest doubt that you have pulled one of history's greatest con games on the country that you called the greatest in the world.

THE FRAUD

Yeah, tell me something I haven't heard before. Tell me something new. You mean the questions about my ineligibility to be President? All kinds of Neocons, reactionaries, and Republicans have been trying to hang that one on me, and every last one of them has failed. So, next evidence, if you please.

THE FASCIST

Not so fast. Let us do you a favor and present you the evidence. Believe us, it is good, very good, and it will assuredly cost you your job, every penny you may have, and even your testicles.

THE FRAUD

Ouch! You can talk about losing me my job, even every penny I have, but not losing my balls. They are off the table—and *under* it, in a secure pair of pants!

Okay, let me hear your evidence. You had a hilarious laugh a minute ago. It is my turn to have one too.

THE FASCIST

At your service. But, you have to relax, if you can, and sit back and listen. We will give you only a synopsis of the evidence, so we do not tax your thin patience that you warned us about. We are your friends, and we want to stay your friends. And a real friend should never do anything that hurts a friend.

I cringed when I watched such blatant and obvious sucking up by the wretch, as it was embarrassingly transparent. The bogus Kumbaya boy continued.

THE FASCIST

You just told us that you know all about those villains who have tried but failed to nail you on this birth-certificate thing. Maybe you are still playing games with me, or maybe you are too busy puffing up your chest with pride in yourself to notice some very damning evidence. I certainly would not be making a monkey of myself by simply re-hashing some unsubstantiated innuendo, would I?

THE FRAUD

No, I am sure you wouldn't make a monkey of yourself. Particularly not a monkey anyway, since it is one of the most common names your enemies call you. You don't want to wear that, do you?

THE FASCIST

No, I do not. Speaking of wearing, it sure looks like before you know it, you will be wearing something much worse, a sort of government-issue attire, that is. To give you a hint, it is not a military uniform. But, let me stick to the present point.

Ever heard of a man named Gary Kreep? Does it not ring a bell? Gary Kreep is a point-man for a group called United States Justice Foundation. You still cannot connect? Kreep reports that you have spent $950,000 in campaign funds in the past year with 11 law firms in 12 states for legal work to block disclosure of any of your personal record. Now, if you did not have something terribly incriminating to hide, why would you pay all that money and go to all that trouble to hide your record? What is wrong with showing a birth certificate? Even though my enemies claim I'm really Jewish, I still show my proof. You and everyone else in the world are welcome to see it.

The big-nosed loud-mouth held up what looked like his passport, something he had done for the press after voting in a past election. I recalled with an ironic smile that a genealogy expert had insisted that the Fascist's real last name, Sabourjian, was that of a family of Jewish *weavers.*

THE FRAUD

Groan. Please stop with the "Birther" rubbish! So, what else do you have to say besides a bunch of bullcrap made up by *my* enemies? Heck, for all I know, *you* made it up, like you probably did the other junk I've already refuted—in fact, I've been wondering where all this garbage is coming from, and now I'm pretty sure it *is* you. Now I have to wonder *why*, since we're both working for the Ummah.

I know who that Kreep creep is, but even *he* has debunked that story. You're just looking for whatever dirt you can find, eh? This competition is a little over the top, you know. How are we supposed to work together if you just repeat a bunch of baloney? What else have you heard, Mr. Gossip?

THE FASCIST

Ah, but you are currently working for the wrong part of the Ummah—we do not consider those Sunni heretics to be true believers.

Anyway, they say that your Attorney General Holder, in tandem with you, dispatched teams of Federal lawyers by the droves at the taxpayers' expense to various courts to prevent people from digging your dirt out.

Only a couple more things should do it for now. First, two Kenyan government ministers have stated in the Kenyan parliament that you were indeed born in Kenya. One of them went as far as demanding that you be repatriated to your country of birth, Kenya. You know the Kenyan minister of lands, James Orengo?

Dozens of other Kenyans, some of them your own blood relatives, have confirmed the fact of your birth in Kenya. And your birth certificate must indeed show that—that is why you are doing all you can to prevent it from surfacing. But, believe me it *will* surface. Mark my words.

The second piece of evidence comes from your undergraduate file. Americans for Freedom of Information has released copies of your college transcripts from Occidental College. Remember the place? The transcript shows that you, under the name of "Barry Soetoro," received financial aid as a foreign student from Indonesia while an undergraduate at the school. You are Barry Soetoro, presently going by the name of Barrack Obama, leaving that blessed name of Hussein out to please the Zionist-Christian cabal, right? The transcript was released by Occidental College in compliance with a court order in a suit brought by the group in the Superior Court of California. As your brother, it makes us shudder to think of your very near bleak future, shuttling from one court to one law office and eventually ending up in an eight-by-eight cell as a guest of the government you presently head, for the rest of your life—

THE FRAUD

Stop shuddering for me, and get to the bottom of it, will you? So you've got some crazy Kenyans talkin' trash—do they have any real proof? Of course they want to claim I'm a Kenyan citizen—I'm the most famous person of Kenyan descent in a long time. It's good for business. That bogus AFI organization you mention doesn't even exist, and you haven't seen any evidence that I went to school under the name of Soetero—because it doesn't exist. Do you just repeat every unsubstantiated rumor you hear? Your intel is not very good, dude.

THE FASCIST

We will continue with the evidence, whether or not it is valid, as it makes for good disinformation to keep people confused. Anyway, the transcript shows that you applied for financial aid and were awarded a fellowship for foreign students from the Fulbright Foundation Scholarship program. To qualify for this scholarship, a student must claim foreign citizenship. I am beginning to think that those who keep calling you fraud have a case—

THE FRAUD

Okay, okay, so just more bullcrap—my transcripts have never been released. You yourself just said that I paid a lot of money to keep my records secret. So which is it?

Anyway, I admit the fact that I was born to an American mother and a Kenyan father, and I was still a babe when my mom took me back to the States. Later, she married an Indonesian, and we moved to Indonesia—yeah, I studied Islam there. So, what's the big deal...?

THE FASCIST

Well, then, do they not have reason to wonder about your background when no records have been released or are forthcoming, as you claim?

To you, it sounds like quibbling about nothing. But an awful lot of Americans are incensed at you screwing them and violating a cardinal provision of America's Constitution—the constitution that you swore on the Bible to uphold and protect. And that is the big deal, my friend. They say you *are* a Manchurian Candidate—and working with the Muslim Brotherhood, which, again, is a Mossad front.

THE FRAUD

Ha! So are you a Manchurian Candidate and a fraud. So was GWB—aren't we all?

Anyway, let's pretend for a minute that those crazy Kenyans are right, and I *was* born in Kenya—not that I think that's any big deal, since my mom was American. But, where do we go from here, just in case?

THE FASCIST

At the risk of quibbling, what you allegedly have done—not being a real American citizen but serving as President—is not a simple infraction. It is a major criminal offense.

There are times that you amaze me. You do not seem to get it, or you are trying to screw me too? You make me repeat myself. Look, those country bumpkins you charmed in Iowa, together with a legion of ACORN louts, got you the nomination. And people were so sick of George Dubbah-you—did I say that right?—that they did not want his geriatric political clone McCain to replace him. So, you got in. Now, they are wising up that you are another one of the same elite group, an internationalist, not an "American," *per se.*

The common people are beginning to see you for what you are, and come 2012 they are likely to throw you on your arse in the street. Most likely, people such as Kreep will get more court orders forcing you to release the original of your birth certificate, not the copy things you have been handing out. And that will be the most damning smoking gun, and the slammer will be your next residence, as we said earlier.

You will not be re-elected in 2012. Mark my word. In fact, you will not even get re-nominated by your own party. You know that little woman you beat in the primaries, the same woman you keep dispatching to every corner of the world to have her out of your way, named Hillary? She will lead the charge for your testicles. But relax, all is not lost. We have good news for you...

After this thorough thrashing—half of which might be true, if we could trust that blatant liar, but which was vehemently denied by the Fraud—the Fascist obviously believed he had his "internationalist" counterpart like putty in his hands. He had him right where he wanted him. In any case, whoever was right, it certainly was amusing being a fly on the wall!

THE FRAUD

> Why do I have this nagging feeling that the good news you are referring to is all for you? Is it out of your charitable heart that you want to help me? I mean, we know one another too well to go for that kind of crap... And, of course, you want me to work for you instead of the Muslim Brotherhood.

THE FASCIST

> You are absolutely correct. It is no charity at all, what we plan to offer you. It is a cool, calculated, win-win business transaction. Just bear with us. Let us have a glass or two in celebration, rinse our mouth thoroughly to wash off all the bad taste of the present discourse as well as any remnants of the satanic brew, face Mecca and offer our from-the-heart prayers of gratitude. We promise you, you would love what we have to offer you in return for your cooperation.

> Just to end the session on a high note, we assure you that there is an excellent way out. Before the U.S. marshals march you into court handcuffed and shackled like a common criminal, you catch the first plane to Tehran, and we will set you up with all the amenities that your heart desires. We shall explain the details in a jiffy. Now, let us get on with our celebration.

Act Eleven

*G*lasses of Scotch Whisky and the finest Shiraz *wine washed down, mouths thoroughly rinsed, earnest prayers ether-mailed to Mecca, the two wheeler-dealers got down to business. Although both still a bit woozy from the intoxicants, they seemed functional enough to continue the horse-trading.*

THE FASCIST

> We recall your earlier expression—the one about being a practical man and wanting to know exactly what things we can do and offer that would improve on what you are and what you have. We hope that you are convinced, if not alarmed, by your not-too-comforting prospects. Your abode could consist of a windowless solitary cell of a Federal prison, denied even the privilege of conjugal visits by your *manzel*—

THE FRAUD

> Hey, I thought we were done with the bad part, and you were going to tell me about the good part. What's this crap talk about a solitary cell and no conjugal visits?

THE FASCIST

> Yes, thank you for reminding us. We should focus on the good news. You need to get your head out of the sand, have your big ears tuned to the max and your eyes wide open. The minute you detect that the dogs are closing in on your tail, you bail out. As I said, you catch the first plane to Tehran, and a life of charm will be waiting for you.

THE FRAUD

> Are you still under the influence of what we imbibed? I noticed that you also *swallowed* some of your medications with the wine. So, you smoke the stuff, and you also *eat* it? You remind me of Edgar Allen Poe. They say he was an opium eater.

THE FASCIST

> We take our medication whichever way we can. Smoking it calms us gradually and keeps on taking us higher and higher and for as high as we wish to go. Eating it is a one-shot thing, and depending on what else is in our gastrointestinal tract, the effect varies. By the way, Edgar Allen Poe took it both ways also. Now, back to what we were saying...

THE FRAUD

> Right, right. I take the first plane and haul my high-tail to Tehran to start a life of charm. I hope you don't mean that's *all* I get when I hightail it to Tehran—the charm of *your* company? What would I be doing? Are you getting tired of your present attendant, and would I be his replacement?

THE FASCIST

My advice—do not quit your day job. You will never make it as a comedian. A clown maybe, but not a comedian.

THE FRAUD

Well, maybe we can team up. You know, like Bob Hope and Bing Crosby. They made it and made it good. You and I, what do you say? We go on a world tour.

THE FASCIST

Pray tell me, now who is the one who is suffering from the after-effects of what we imbibed?

THE FRAUD

Okay, this round goes to you. You are such a disarming little fellow, aren't you?

THE FASCIST

My stature is none of your business. Besides, do not let that fool you. We match and even beat yours by inches. What you do not see about us, I mean.

THE FRAUD

Another round to you. You're doing all the winning. Am I going to win anything?

THE FASCIST

If you would only shut your mouth and open up your big ears wider, we will tell you and gladden your heart. So, listen good.

THE FRAUD

Mum's the word. I'm all ears.

THE FASCIST

We believe the "ear" part.

The foul howler let out another one of his deathly hyena laughs while the internationalist chameleon covered his ears in mock protest.

THE FRAUD

Okay, so I land at Tehran's new Imam Khomeini International Airport. What's next?

THE FASCIST

Next is a whole slew of great things. No, we are not tired of our attendant, and we do not plan to waste our time training you for the job. You are destined for another line of work—

THE FRAUD

Got it. I'll be your political advisor, right?

THE FASCIST

Close, but not on target. What happened to your promise of shutting up and listening good? Do you or do you not want to hear what I am going to say?

THE FRAUD

Breathlessly, I do.

THE FASCIST

You will be received by the country's highest dignitaries. As a matter of fact, I have the word of his Eminence—the Supreme Leader Ali Khamenei—that he himself will be the lead dignitary to welcome you. You will be his personal guest for seven days, during which time anybody who is anybody from the ranks of the clergy, civil servants and the military will be presented to you—

THE FRAUD

I know, I know—I'm again violating my pledge by not staying mum. This is so enthralling already that I can't contain myself—just kidding. I have a question. Why wait until the dogs you referred to nip at my tail? But, seriously, why not just do it right now?

THE FASCIST

Hold off, man. Not so fast. Remember, this is a business transaction. In any business transaction, the parties must exchange goods, services or money. We are not offering all this to you from the goodness of our heart, we are sure you can appreciate that. We also want something from you. But, let me assure you what we are offering you for your part is by far of greater benefit to you. You will come out way ahead, believe me.

THE FRAUD

Okay, I'll try to stay quiet and hear you out. Go ahead.

THE FASCIST

A week of welcome and festivities behind you, you will be escorted by a motorcade to the holy city of Qom—

THE FRAUD

Hey, you just poured a bucket of piss on my fire. That God-forsaken dump in the middle of an abominable desert is the last place on earth I want to go. Your Tehran with its smoggy air that makes Los Angeles's appear like pure oxygen by comparison is bad enough. Qom? It even makes the Federal prison you predicted for me look not all that bad. No, no Qom— that's the same "holy" hellhole where officials from your Department of Justice and other governmental agencies were arrested when a mullah-operated prostitution ring was busted up. Forget it. The deal is off—

THE FASCIST

Calm down. Hear us out. We promise you would like it. We mean, you would like the *package* deal. Calm down.

THE FRAUD

Okay, I'll try, but I won't promise.

THE FASCIST

Just to help calm you down, I will get ahead of myself. Qom—which has a lovely mosque, you know—will be your official place of residence, but not the actual place. And we will explain for you the reasons. You will have your own private jet with a complete complement of personnel to service any and all needs that your heart desires. You can, on a moment's notice, fly to the fully-staffed Caspian resort that will be at your disposal. Or you can spend as much time as you like in the many mountainous resorts of the magnificent Alborz range. Literally, the sky is the limit, as the saying goes.

THE FRAUD

Hey, that sounds better. But tell me what a man like me will be doing in a place like Qom? That place is a religious town from end to end. It is a two-industry town. It imports untold thousands of the dead who want to be buried there and exports untold thousands of mullahs to feed the masses phony religious staples until they die. And me, I'm a wrong fit for it—

THE FASCIST

Do not worry. We will fit you without a hitch. Besides, it would be the greatest thing for our holy faith short of the advent of His Blessedness, the Sahib al-Zaman—

THE FRAUD

And here I thought that I'd climbed as high as any man could ever aspire to climb. And you're telling me that something bigger and greater is in store for me?

THE FASCIST

We are telling you exactly that, and we are dead serious. No, do not look at us like that. And no, neither the satanic brew nor the medication is doing the talking. It is a "straight poop," as you people say...

THE FRAUD

It does strangely reek like one. Yet, I certainly hope it's not. No poop, straight or otherwise, please.

THE FASCIST

Speaking of poop, we must attend to it right this minute. We are sure you do not mind a short recess, do you?

THE FRAUD

No, not at all. Poop time it is, for me too.

And here I thought the two nutcases were pooping all along. Go figure.

Act Twelve

 *ith the anal poop out of the two poopers, oral poop began to flow once again. And the short in stature but long in poop started the flow.*

THE FASCIST

My esteemed guest, you are going to like this deal. You really are. I wish it was me instead of you. I truly mean that—

THE FRAUD

Tell you what. I'm a generous guy. If it's such an irresistible prize that you, my dear friend, wish to have it, it's yours. Take it. It pleases me to no end to have you take it. What do you say? See, I'm a real pal. Don't give me that look. You don't believe I'm a very generous man? Well, didn't I give my Nobel Peace Prize money to charity? Didn't keep a nickel of it, did I? My generosity is on public record.

THE FASCIST

Thanks for nothing. That Nobel Peace Prize actually should be re-named "*Ignoble Piss Prize,*" with recipients like you and that loud-mouth, no-good woman, Shirin Ebadi. Never mind her. She is not at issue right now. But you, Mr. Laureate, what in hell did you accomplish to deserve the prize? If my memory serves me right, you had not even finished a carton of your cigarettes as President, much less having done anything else, when the Euronut liberals nominated you for the prize, right? Then—voila!—just like that, a couple of months later you were announced the winner. Now, tell me, did it not embarrass you going there and accepting the prize that you had not done a piss to earn? I know, I know. That is the story of your life. Like during the few years that you were a United States senator—you did not sponsor even a single legislation, did you? All you did was to feather your nest, write those glib books, and scheme.

Believe me, those are great qualities that we deeply admire in you. They are needed to navigate through the treacherous terrain of the present world until the Sahib al-Zaman appears and sets things aright.

THE FRAUD

You're way too rude, dude, so thanks for the offer—but, no thanks! We shall take that as an I.O.U. to cash in the future. Why the decline of your offer? It just ain't a good fit.

THE FASCIST

It is custom made for you and only you. His Eminence himself proposed the plan after a recent visit he paid to the holy precinct of the Sahib al-Zaman at Jamkaran. It was there, offering prayer at the mouth of the well, believe it or not, that the plan was revealed to him. I know that sounds creepy to creeps. But you are a lover of Islam, and that is the beauty of being a true believer, such that no satanic machination will make you doubt the reality of faith.

Now, just think about it—a priceless fringe benefit of your new position is that Jamkaran is within a short hop from Qom. You can visit that hallowed spot as often as your heart desires—

THE FRAUD

I can't tell what my heart's desire will be like in the future. But, right this minute my heart's burning desire is to get the hell out of here and forget all about you and the fact that we ever met—

THE FASCIST

The more you bitch about the whole thing, the more will be your regret once you find out what a magnificent deal you are being offered. Once again, we request that you refrain from throwing your very sickening temper tantrums, and stop getting angry. Bring to mind what Mark Twain said about anger—it is a gem. He said, when angry count to three, when very angry count to 10. I guess it is too much to ask you to count to 10. It demands too much math from you. But try to count to three before you express your anger, and allow us to spell it out for you.

THE FRAUD

On one condition. Don't use that damned term, "Spell it out." Hearing it makes me spell out whatever is still in my system. Okay, don't use it? Just go ahead and tell me.

THE FASCIST

You do not have a monopoly on generosity, so, request granted. We shan't be using that term again, unless you are in need of an emetic.

Then he barked another one of his thunderous howls that had started making me feel the way the Fraud felt hearing the "spell it out" phrase. I finally found a way of dealing with that: Each time he started his hyena howl, I pushed the mute button on the remote, since I couldn't tell the creep to stop it. I can't be sure what was so funny, but I noticed the loser's use of "shan't." Perhaps flaunting his mastery of British English? Or was the use of the word "emetic"—which describes a substance ingested to bring on vomiting—showing off his medical acumen? Your guess is as good as mine. After a long minute, he went on.

THE FASCIST

We set you up in Qom as an ayatollah—

THE FRAUD

Come on, man. Don't sh— me. I don't have to count even to three. I'm mad. This is all crap. I'm getting out of here. I've had it with you.

With that, the irate internationalist got up to leave. The Fascist jumped to his feet and grabbed him by the thigh, since he couldn't reach much farther, I suppose, and pleaded with him to hear him out. The Fraud, still fuming, reluctantly returned to his seat with murder in his eyes. I suppose if it were not for the fear of the Thick Thug, he would've squashed the little bug into a hash of flesh and sh—.

THE FASCIST

Sorry. Did we shock you? Well, we were complying with your request to get to the point. And honestly, that is the point. You will become, in no time at all, the most revered ayatollah in the world. Just hear us out. See, we did not use that phrase that you asked us not to.

We feel the need for a brief recess to refresh ourselves, and start the next session with the wonderful news that we have in store for you. What do you say?

THE FRAUD

> Wow, this is the first time that you actually asked *my* opinion. Maybe you have some good news for me, although I very much doubt it. I recall a Farsi proverb I read that went something like this: "What oozes from a jug is what's in it." And from the kind of jug that you are only that which is in you can ooze. Need I say more?

This round went to the Fraud. He laughed for several moments.

Act Thirteen

*O*nce again the two assumed their respective cushions on the floor and began to ooze. Incidentally, the word "ooze" sounds much like "goose," and the word "goose" in Farsi means "audible digestive gas"—exactly what these two had been doing during their meetings. I couldn't resist the urge to share with you this illuminating editorial comment.

THE FRAUD

Okay, so I'm an ayatollah. Why aren't you coming and kissing my feet, or at least my hand?

THE FASCIST

See what a little wine and medication can do? Put us in a good mood. And what you just said will indeed happen. We will be doing just that in public, but not just yet. Even then, we will whip your butt in private, when and if the two of us are alone and unobserved. We are sure that, knowing what a coward you are, you will see to it that we do not catch you unattended by one or more of your legion of flunkies—

THE FRAUD

Get to the point and try to ooze something better. Tell me how am I going to be masquerading as ayatollah when I don't know sh— about even some of the obvious points of our faith and am completely at sea when it comes to the very abstruse stuff that constitutes the turf of the most learned? Do I have to write a dissertation on some very obscure yet important aspect of the faith that no one else had elucidated? I mean, like what your Shi'a saint, the late Ayatollah Khomeini, did?

What earned Khomeini his unsurpassed status as not only Grand Ayatollah but also Imam was Khomeini's detailed and brilliant discourse on the "do's and don'ts" of sexual intercourse with all kinds of animals, ranging from chickens to elephants—in his infamous *Little Green Book*, right? There is nothing of significance left for me, the know-nothing, to elucidate and earn my standing. And don't tell me I can write my dissertation on intercourse with insects since the great Imam didn't cover that area.

THE FASCIST

You are funny, in a sick kind of way. We grant you that. Our advice? Keep these stupid thoughts to yourself and do not ever breathe a word that would remotely question, much less ridicule, the late Point of Emulation, Imam Khomeini.

THE FRAUD

Well, I haven't signed on yet, have I? It's better for me to raise these concerns now before two-bit fascists like you fasten a muzzle around my mouth—

THE FASCIST

Thanks for bringing that up—and for the hostility, which gives us cause now to show our true, rude face, regardless of our brotherhood! As the Holy Quran says, "Fight for the sake of Allah those that fight against you, but do not attack them first. Allah does not love the aggressors." Since you are a Sunni heretic and not yet a real Muslim, and since you have just attacked us, we are now free to attack you back. But, using other verses, we attack others first anyway, so do not hold me to that! You do know about the Mecca-Medina division of the holy scriptures and how the later verses abrogate the earlier ones, when it is convenient to us?

Anyway, although you are clearly the Chosen One for our plan of global domination, we need to order an extra large muzzle for your big mouth. For now, let us use a virtual muzzle— keep your yap shut so we can proceed.

And now let us focus on the business of making an ayatollah out of you. It is a breath of fresh air to hear you admit your ignorance. We will give you that. We have your dissertation already done, ready for your delivery at a gathering of the land's top ayatollahs so with your oratory you can mesmerize them. See how it works? You look puzzled. I will explain.

Your true identity will be revealed to the world. You have been ever since childhood a devoted Muslim—whether or not you agree, that is Islamic law: Your father is a Muslim, you are a Muslim, although, again, you are a heretic. But we can change that. Here is the story we will tell:

Unbeknownst to the stupid and ignorant masses, at the age of eight while still in Indonesia, after having said your prayers one early dawn, a luminous being of magnificent bearing and beauty, sporting a beard and wearing a green turban, embraced you. You felt an indescribably glorious ecstasy in his embrace, and you wished that you could remain there forever. This luminous visitor was none other than the much-prayed-for Sahib al-Zaman. He spoke to you some immortal words that you have never forgotten. Are you with me?

THE FRAUD

Yeah, but I wish I was anywhere else but here. Keep oozing. It makes for a dime-novel worth of fiction that I can hawk to the millions of gullible Shi'ites who buy any and all crap of this sort.

THE FASCIST

Watch your language. We may have to have our attendant do something about that tongue of yours. The only thing that is holding us back from so doing is that filthy tongue of yours is needed for a greater purpose. Recall that in our holy faith, lofty ends justify any and all means. That is why we are explicitly instructed in the scripture to employ our holy deception, *taqiyya,* along with *kitman*, which is how we hide our Muslim faith in order to advance our cause of jihad and global domination.

THE FRAUD

If I were a Sunni—and I'm not saying I am—I would not be able to use *taqiyya*, but even if I did, I would still *honestly* say at the moment that, once again, I'm itching to get the hell out of here. And this time, don't grab my thigh. You might contact my privates, and I don't like to be touched there by whiskered creeps like you. I've seen the way you kiss other men—all the while claiming there are no homos in Iran. Did you honestly believe I could forget those horrible images of you liplocked with *guys*?

THE FASCIST

> Go ahead and insult us. And do not pretend
> those Sunni heretics do not use *taqiyya*—they
> just call it by a different word: "Negotiation."
> Again, we put up with you Sunni back-alley
> trash only because we have a plan where you
> are—worthless as you may be—pivotal to its
> success. His Eminence will have my balls fed to
> me on a kebab skewer if I fail in my mission.

> And as to my public kissing and hand-holding
> with men, I have got two words for you: "Larry
> Sinclair." Yes, we know all about that little
> scandal—did you think we were not paying
> attention, Mr. Down Low? You cannot criticize
> us for our latent homosexuality, can you? What
> about Donald Young?

*At these words, the Fraud's head snapped to attention,
and he stared in horror and shock at the little man
enthroned in front of him. After a moment, the
American-Internationalist regained his composure and
addressed the Islamist tyrant.*

THE FRAUD

> Egads. You're the most gossipy person I've ever
> met—worse than the womenfolk in my family.
> Are you going to raise *all* the rubbish ever
> thrown at me? Where's your proof? Is this why
> you asked me here? Maybe I should leave just
> now, so you end up actually eating your own
> charbroiled balls.

*This time, it was the Fraud's turn to double up with
laughter, a laughter that was second only to that of the
Fascist in vulgarity. In return, the Fascist looked the
part of a man who had just been sprayed by a skunk. It
served him well and delighted me. I have to print, in
due time, images of his face. It's so expressive, it makes
the word "revolting" seem a compliment by comparison.*

THE FASCIST

As we were saying to you, you ungrateful S.O.B., we make sure that the entire thing is on a teleprompter so you do not end up scratching your behind searching for words. It will all be there in front of your shifty eyes. With your oratory and added command of Arabic, it is a cinch. You will bring those fat-ass, do-nothing leeches to their feet—

THE FRAUD

Hey, explain that first. I thought you revered those bloodsuckers, now that I am going to be one of them?

THE FASCIST

Yes, in this land of ours what you see is usually not what is or what you get. There is a great deal of smoke-and-mirrors kind of thing. Only the devoted believers of the Sahib al-Zaman can see through the charade, play the game, while all along carrying out His Blessedness's orders. We put up with those wolves, because they still command the loyalty of the masses of illiterates and semi-literates. We need them, and we use them, as they use us. They get their free ride on the back of the ignorant public, while we gallop forward with our assignments. In this world, those are the facts on the ground. It is no different in America. Only there, it is the Zionists in charge, while the politicians ride.

THE FRAUD

God, you're good, very savvy. Tell you what. You're wasted here in Iran working for the guy who has the power of feeding you your balls. And my CIA boys tell me that the great majority of Iranians also would love nothing better than to feed Seyyed Ali Khamenei, the Supreme

Leader, his *own* balls on a skewer. It's the same kind of treat he keeps promising you. Why don't *you* bolt and come to America as a political refugee? As the President, I'll see to it you get a bodyguard around the clock, some stipend for the rest of your life, and no one will ever be in a position of feeding you your balls. Somehow, I can't get that balls feeding thought out of my head—

THE FASCIST

Do try. Our pledge is with the Sahib al-Zaman. We are his eternal vessel. No worldly incentive or threat can ever shake our resolve to carry out his orders. Need we remind you that we are in personal communication with him, that we long to carry out whatever he commands to hasten his appearance, and no promise or threat is capable of swaying us from our sacred mission.

THE FRAUD

I'll give you that—that's loyalty. So, you decline the offer? Then go ahead tell me the rest.

THE FASCIST

And ever since that momentous childhood event when you had the vision of the Sahib al-Zaman, you secretly switched to the true Islam, although in obedience to the dictates of our faith you exercised both *taqiyya* and *kitman* to work most effectively for His Blessedness—

THE FRAUD

Wait a minute, man. You're mixing water and oil. On the one hand, you are saying that we are working for the Pure Twelfth Imam, the Hidden One. He is supposed to be a paragon of all the virtues that are so alien to you and me. On the other hand, you say that we should go

ahead with this farce of a fraud to further his
agenda—is that deception *virtuous*? I don't get
it.

THE FASCIST

Glad to see you admit your befuddlement. That
is why we are here, remember? We will gladly
take all the time needed to dispel any doubt or
answer any question that you may have. We
are not mixing water and oil, as you put it.
What we *are* doing is to do whatever it takes,
using any and all means, good, bad, or
anything in between, to achieve the objective.
Do we need to remind you that it is the sacred
duty of the true believer to use whatever it
takes to further the realization of mankind's
perennial prayer—making this bowl of dust,
earth, a reflection of heaven? Surely, when a
structure decays, you take a steel wrecking ball
to it. You tear it down, clear the ground and
ready it for the new edifice. You do not fret
about how you tear it down, do you?

THE FRAUD

Oops. I was just about to say that you make
the celebrated the Blessed One a second-rate
mind compared to you. But, I didn't mention
him by name just to show you that I am
reciprocating your kindness of not using that
phrase that I do abhor when you want to
explain something—

THE FASCIST

Stop speaking in riddles. As we were saying,
ever since that magnificent encounter with the
Sahib al-Zaman, without you even knowing it,
you began to implement the assignments that
he personally began handing to you all along.
He urged you to study the language of the
revelation and to master it. He wished you to

immerse yourself in studying the Quran and all the scriptures. And he urged you to maintain complete secrecy in all your affairs. By the way, we must commend you for doing all that. We are particularly impressed by how successfully you have been able to cover your true identity from the American public. To this day, even your closest associates are not sure they know much about the real you—and they *do not*. That is truly commendable—it's what we admire about you, although practically the only thing.

THE FRAUD

Thanks. Frankly, I myself don't know who I really am. And you are here now trying to do a major re-make on me. I'm not sure that I will like it, but I'm beginning to gravitate to it. It's intriguing—I mean, this whole world is a stage, as Shakespeare said, and the people are the actors. I say, why not? If you fit the role, and it's exciting, you might as well go ahead and assume it, right?

THE FASCIST

Yes and no. You might look at it that way. Not us. We are not a role-player. We are for real and are not implementing a script written by some joker but, rather, executing a plan ordained by Allah Himself and relayed to us by our adoring superior, the Sahib al-Zaman, who speaks to us from his well.

THE FRAUD

You keep mentioning the Sahib al-Zaman so frequently that I am beginning to feel the same way about him as I do about the other phrase. Would you please economize in using the name of your imaginary friend? I mean, if I'm also going to be pretending to work for him, I don't want to puke every time I hear his name, do I?

THE FASCIST

You are a repugnant trash even thinking such thoughts. Yet, we forgive you for your impudence talking like that. We have, in our path of service to the Beloved, suffered greater indignities than your blasphemous speech. We pray to him to give us the strength to deal with excrement like you.

I could see that the little tyrant was very much enjoying this ability to deprecate the President of the United States, even if they were brothers in faith, because the Fraud was still just a filthy Sunni heretic and kafir.

THE FRAUD

Okay, which am I, ayatollah or excrement? Are you telling me they are one and the same?

THE FASCIST

In your case and in the case of many ayatollahs, they *are* one and the same. Question answered, let me proceed.

THE FRAUD

Permission granted. Proceed.

THE FASCIST

Once you are acclaimed as the miraculous handiwork of you-know-who—we are not using his blessed name in compliance with your request—we will set you up with your own seminary where a bevy of eager students will vie with one another to study at your feet.

THE FRAUD

Yeah, that doesn't turn me on, man. A bunch of bearded, smelly aspiring leeches who don't take a bath from week to week crowding around me—to learn what?

THE FASCIST

Calm down. Keep in mind the alternative that assuredly awaits you—an eight-by-eight concrete cell with blank walls, no windows and heavy iron gates in a Federal prison. Or, perhaps, some zealous brother will take serious issue with your blatant apostasy. You are, my friend, between a rock and a hard place. The bearded stinking students crowding around your own stinking feet should look pretty attractive by comparison.

THE FASCIST

You still didn't answer my question. I don't know sh— about this stuff. What would I be teaching these leeches and wanabees? Will some ayatollah be teaching from behind a curtain, and I just mouth the words? That's not exactly the kind of titillating life I have in mind.

THE FASCIST

Do not be a simpleton. We know you are not that bright, your Fulbright and Harvard education notwithstanding, but you do not have to be a complete idiot, do you? Or do you have to take us as morons?

THE FRAUD

You know something, friend? I am still trying my hardest to find out what you actually meant when you said that your proposal is a win-win for *me*—winning in this world and in the next. So far, I haven't seen it.

THE FASCIST

We are a man of our word. We shall deliver what we promised. No, no ayatollah will be pulling your string, although we must admit that you can make a passable puppet the way you have been talking from both sides of your mouth, mostly broadcasting meaningless banalities and getting away with it.

THE FRAUD

Yeah, I got it. That's what I am good at. Broadcasting banality is what I'll be doing in my seminary?

THE FASCIST

Bravo. Close. Very close. The broadcasting part is right on target. You will have your specialty subject. You do not have to breathe one solitary word about abstruse theological issues. If anyone presents you with a question of the sort, you brush it aside. If you have to deal with it, you relegate the matter to one of your many underling mullahs to address it. You are completely focused on devoting yourself to the urgent matters of your assignments from On High—see, I didn't refer to him by name—to be sidetracked. The master faker that you are, that should present no problem, should it?

THE FRAUD

I suppose not. It still sounds like a zany idea, but less so. I'm listening.

THE FASCIST

Good. You are coming around to see the beauty of it in a minute, and you will really love it. It fits you to a "t," as the saying goes.

THE FRAUD

Okay, move on and stop all those cute expressions that you have packed in your full-of-you-know-what cranium.

THE FASCIST

> Hey, I am doing you an immense favor. I am
> rescuing you from certain prison and possible
> death, and giving you the kind of life that
> people much worthier than you would kill for.
> So, be grateful and more respectful to me. It is
> only decent to do that, but you would not know
> what decency is anyway.

THE FRAUD

> Right. Neither one of us knows or has any use
> for decency. Just like truth. Let's bury that
> next to truth and never mention them. What we
> are embarking on clashes head on with useless
> concepts like those. However, I'll try my best
> not to call you what you really are, provided
> that you don't provoke me too much.

> Tell me now. What is my specialty subject and
> what is my assignment from down low? Sorry, I
> meant from "On High," but since it is coming
> from you it must be coming from down low—or
> should I say, "lowlife?"

THE FASCIST

> Being a comedian, you are not. Being a jerk,
> you are. Yet, you have to transcend your
> garbage self and serve as an instrument of his
> blessed will. Specifically, you broadcast, as you
> used the term, all the evils of the Great Satan
> in detail, without letup. An entire cadre of
> writers will supply you with material daily. And
> you, for your part, will be a most credible
> mouthpiece. Do you see that? It is brilliant.
> You have worked your way up every step of the
> cesspool of the infidel world, and you have seen
> it all first hand. All along you took part as a
> sort of what sociologists call "participant
> observer," to see and document the corruption,
> horror and filth of the *kafir* world. And having

reached the very apex and completed your findings, you have taken it upon yourself to expose it and invite the world into the one-and-only tabernacle of salvation—the faith of Twelve Imamate Islam, the Twelver Shi'a religion.

How do you like it? Don't you just love it? We told you that you are the perfect fit for it, didn't we?

THE FRAUD

Yeah, I suppose so. I could do that. But I still have some nagging concerns...

THE FASCIST

A nag, you sure have been. Do not stop now and nag. What is bothering you?

THE FRAUD

For one, earlier I mentioned this in passing—all these grandiose schemes assume that Seyyed Ali, you and your gang of fanatics are not going to be dangling from tree limbs and lampposts before long. Do you remember the millions of people who flocked to the streets of your major cities after the last thieving election that got you into office? Those people are still there. Although many of them, the best young brains of the country, are leaving the prison you call the Islamic Republic of Iran the first chance they get. With those people on the loose, your hold is tenuous at best, the way I see it—

THE FASCIST

Your vision is as bad as the stuff behind it. Our hold on power is not only stable, it is ironclad. We told you earlier. We are realists—and a dedicated group of realists with a mission. We do not give a rat's feces about the few brats of Northern Tehran. Pampered children of the rich, that is what they are. The minute our brave Basij—the volunteer militia founded by Imam Khomeini—go boo, those boys and girls start running as if the devil himself were after them. A handful that doesn't scram fast enough, we catch and take them as our guests for a few days of hospitality. Just for added measure, our men see to it that half a dozen or so don't get to find their way home. The rest get the message, loud and clear. We limit those worthless mama's boys and girls to barking slogans within the sanctuary of the universities, where we let them scream themselves hoarse while feeling good about themselves. *Millions* of them, you say they are? My attendant's butt, that is what I say. You must be watching selective and highly doctored clips the Zionists feed you.

Besides, what do run-of-the-mill people know, anyway? Democracy and republic are euphemisms at best. You like that term, "euphemism?" Do you know what it means? Or did not your Harvard education press your soft brains with heavy words like that?

THE FRAUD

What I'd like is to be relieved from being caged with the most disgusting creature I have ever had the misfortune of running into. Yeah, I'm impressed with your command of English and your first-rate conniving, double-crossing, rotten mind. Do you want me to put that in writing so you can get on with it?

THE FASCIST

No, you do not have to put it in writing. Just seeing you squirm is a delicious experience, only second to putting a bullet into your worthless head. As you pointed out, we have done that more than a few times. What we never told you is how much we truly enjoyed doing it.

The sadistic speech was not unexpected but remained sickening. I thought the sudden outburst of insults was strange, but it's quite likely these two cranks' blood sugar was low from all the partying. Also, as the leader of a regime infamous for torture, the Fascist was well aware that insulting people is one of the first steps in breaking down their resistance to being subjugated. Threats are next, a skill at which fanatical Islamists had become very adept. This is how it all gets started— basically as a bar fight between two street brawlers.

THE FRAUD

You finished insulting me? But are you also finished describing my assignment?

THE FASCIST

Almost. In your seminary, you meet your adoring students on occasions and at your own discretion. No schedules for you, nothing like that. You have complete freedom to run the show as long as you follow the script. We will have all your lectures recorded for broadcast and telecast on all of our stations. We shall also disseminate copies, hard copies as well as videos, to just about every corner of the globe for further use. Are you with us? You catch our drift?

THE FRAUD

I sure hope you yourself drift away. To where? To the inferno of the most dreadful hell, that's where. Get on with it.

THE FASCIST

And you ought to do something about that temper of yours. It would not do for an especially chosen agent of His Blessedness to act and speak out of control. Keep that in mind.

The last major part of your assignment for now is to urge Muslims to devote themselves to the sacred task of jihad prescribed by Rasul Allah. Jihad is so essential to the work of the Beloved. It is even included in the *adhan* or call to prayer that you have said is the most beautiful music to your ear. The *adhan* commands the faithful, *Haya ala al jihad*—"Hasten ye to jihad"—does it not?

But, forget that rubbish about the word "jihad" meaning "inner struggle." We do not struggle with any of our "vices." We just accept them as our natural state and do what we want, when we want it. To us, then, jihad means conquest over the infidel by whatever means—violence works particularly well.

We have many levels of jihad, including stealth jihad, using the infidels' own legal system against them—all of this is commanded by Allah.

THE FRAUD

Undoubtedly, that is how your hypocritical clergy lives their lives, but there are millions of righteous Muslims who disagree—until the likes of you coerce and agitate them.

In any case, speaking of the *adhan*—I'm hearing it now. We must answer it and hurry to perform our prayers.

Without any further ado, the odd couple rushed to answer the call of the adhan.

Act Fourteen

*W*hen the two returned from their long, drawn-out and tedious prayer consisting of umpteen rituals that take far too much time, they sat down as if exhausted and took deep breaths.

THE FASCIST

You look a little glum. Something is wrong?

THE FRAUD

You mean beside the intolerable ordeal of being with you? Yeah, you guessed it. There is something wrong. The deal is off. It's not going to work—

THE FASCIST

Why not? What is the problem? You just told me you were warming up to it and now you want out? What are you, a bipolar-type? Or just the vacillating, spineless worm people say you are?

THE FRAUD

I'll ignore your insults, you imp, simply because you're not even worth a response. But I'll give you the reason anyway: My *manzel*, my wife, will not play. She won't go along.

THE FASCIST

> And that is a problem? Ditch her. Ditch her, and you can have your pick of the best of our women here and as many as your pri— can handle.

THE FRAUD

> No, that's not the problem. The problem is my two daughters. Ditching her is simple enough. I don't particularly get along with that uppity woman. But, she won't come, and she won't let me take custody of my girls.

THE FASCIST

> We wish that you would come up with some difficult problem that we could solve for you since you really do not have the gray cells you need. What concerns you is hardly a problem. Do you want to hear the solution?

THE FRAUD

> Yeah, Mr. Gray Cells—more likely Mr. *Brown* Cells—tell me.

THE FASCIST

> Have you never seen the movie "Not Without My Daughter?" I love that Sally Field—she played the part perfectly, and we were so proud to see our beloved Iran portrayed in such an accurate manner. You see, in the true Islam we do not put up with those bitches who want to turn us all into women—we put them in their place. We *men* take the children, as they are *our* property, not that of those bitches who fight us. Who cares about the mother? She is insignificant. It is the man who matters, always. We pay, we own—it is that simple.

> So the simple solution is, before the dogs nab your tail and before the jig is completely up,

you send your two girls on a little trip. Maybe they go to Hawaii or any place outside the continental United States they want to visit. We will arrange the custody bit with no sweat. We will have our people whisk them away, put them on the next plane, and keep them safe and sound in a most secure place until you get settled, and they will be brought to you.

What is your *manzel* going to do? Go to court and get an extradition order? We need not be graphic and tell you what we do with that piece of paper, although we usually employ water for that purpose. By then, you are the Ayatollah and an honored citizen of the Islamic Republic of Iran where the Islamic laws apply.

Again, under our holy Sharia law it is *fathers*, not mothers, who are the ordained rightful guardians and custodians of their children. Mission accomplished. What will the American government do? Lodge a protest through the Swiss Embassy? Our response: Scram, boys, scram.

Maybe another harebrained moron president, your replacement, decides to send the marines on a rescue mission? Well, he needs to check with Jimmy Carter, the peanut man and as of late America's Apology Ambassador at Large. Ask him about his attempt at rescuing the hostages we held.

When the little ass mentioned President Carter again, I shuddered. In the 1970s, Jimmy Carter actually helped give birth to the virulent Shi'ite Islamism by forbidding the Shah of Iran to crush the bloodthirsty Ayatollah Khomeini and his band of rabid Islamists. Now, the Fraud apparently intended to confer legitimacy on the illegitimate child, the Islamic Republic of Iran.

It was a well-known "secret" among Iranians that Carter's government funded the terrorist Khomeini's *rise, sending $150 million to the ayatollah's bank account in Paris.*

Jimmy Carter did his thing and the Iranian people died. In no time at all, the vicious mullahs gutted the Iranian armed forces and executed many of its most capable officers. Saddam Hussein watched gleefully as the Iranian military disintegrated, and found the opportunity to carry out his Pan Arabism ambition by attacking Iran. Some eight years of barbaric butchery killed and maimed millions on both sides, gutted the vibrant Iranian economy, and visited misery of all sorts upon the Iranian people. Recalling this needless atrocity sickened me, as did the loud-mouth creep sitting in front of me on the screen.

THE FASCIST

If the next president goes ahead and tries that foolishness anyway, he will end up with a bunch of dead marines and a thunderous laugh from all the people who rightfully hate America, with its big swagger and little substance.

Now that I have the floor, let me further sweeten the deal for you. This was not part of our plan—I mean, the plan conceived by the Seyyed. It was just revealed to me from On High during our recess of a few minutes ago. We know that you and I hate each other's guts. But things will play out much better if we do not hate each other, and it will work out excellently if we somehow come up with enough incentives to even like each other—

THE FRAUD

Stop right there. Not a chance! First of all—"We pay, we own?" Are you sure you're not really a Jew? Maybe that news report about your real name "Sabourjian" was right? As you and I both know, there have been many crypto-Jews over the centuries—some say you're one, some say I'm one. I sometimes think everybody's a Jew!

THE FASCIST

Our religion teaches that the Jew hides behind every rock and that Satan is everywhere—

But, not so fast! Hear me out in my proposal. Your two girls are central to the new inspiration I just received from On High. They would make us liking each other possible. You see, it is brilliant: I'll marry both of them—

The American jumped to his feet, neck veins bulging, and waved his fist in the air. His eyes bugged out, and I'd never seen him so angry before.

THE FRAUD

You're such a demented megalomaniac, always believing Allah is speaking to you through one of His representatives. What conceit! What arrogance! I wouldn't even consent to you marrying my dog, much less marrying my two sweeties, you scumbag!

THE FASCIST

Wait! Wait! Just hear me out. His Blessedness, who is assuredly watching our deliberations, put it into my head. Just hear me out, please.

See, you are a consummate Machiavellian with a grease pump. I do not want to call you what others do—"the most unscrupulous sycophant"—but that is what you are. Once you are the Grand Ayatollah, which is a cinch, you unleash your talent of charming, greasing and double-crossing other ayatollahs, as you see fit. I will do whatever you need to have done at my end to facilitate your plan of advancement.

Thanks for letting me finish. See, the Seyyed is both old and in very frail health. He is bound to leave us before long. I mean, he will either be taken by the Blessed One, or the Assembly of Experts will ask him to retire, seeing a brilliant ascending star like you who could give a new lease on the life of the Islamic Republic. Next thing you know, you will be the Supreme Leader! See how beautiful it is? It is not my plan. It is His Blessedness's plan.

THE FRAUD

You must still be under the influence. This is nothing but a pipedream for you!

THE FASCIST

Look, if you do not envision it, you cannot have it, right? No, it is not a pipedream, but I *am* under the influence, the influence of the Blessed One. Everything I do and say is inspiration from him. Have I not repeatedly proclaimed that I am only a vessel for him, that I work for him? You work for the boss, and the boss helps you do the job, right?

With your two daughters as my wives, we will be family. See, how beautiful it is? And we will have both the mosque and the state in the family. Is that not a magnificent plan? Hunh, what do you say?

THE FRAUD

What do I say? Let me repeat myself—it might just get through to your brown cells: I wouldn't even consent to you marrying my dog, much less my two sweeties, you scumbag.

And I am glad you asked me what I say. I have been meaning to say this for a long time and here you prompted me to say it. I say this: If I were Allah's advisor and was allowed only one piece of advice to offer the Merciful One, I would've used my one-and-only chance suggesting He shouldn't create you. Too late, you're already here? Okay, I would've strongly recommended He send you to His inferno, your eternal abode, forthwith.

THE FASCIST

Hey, that is good, very good indeed. So we are not going to become family? We are not going to even get along? I would do a very good job making sure those girls cover and conduct themselves properly—like my wife, who knows her place of subservience—bringing honor to your family. The way you are raising them—I have gazed much at your *manzel's* exposed flesh—your girls will turn out to be typical American prostitutes anyway.

But, alas, are we parting company, then, you on your way to your cell and me to get my balls fed to me by the unforgiving Seyyed?

THE FRAUD

You *would* say such a rotten thing, you sleazebag. If you promise never to talk about my daughters again, I may consent to some parts of your proposal. Not the one about becoming family. That's completely out—and stop looking at my wife's flesh, you ugly bastard. Now I know why you animals have to cover up your women—you just can't control yourselves.

In any case, if I play, I would demand my seminary be next to yours. The unmatched devious conniving S.O.B. that you are can teach me whatever I don't know in treachery and all forms of shenanigans.

THE FASCIST

> We do not have a seminary. We told you that our line of work is in government and not religion. Now who has the thick skull?

THE FRAUD

> I thought in the Islamic Republic, the two are one and the same, a coupling made in heaven.

THE FASCIST

> You thought wrong, and it is not the first time. But in your new position you cannot afford to be the goofball you have been and continue to be. You have to be very circumspect and guarded in your speech. As a matter of fact, you will be so closely scrutinized that you must even muffle the other sound you so often release shamelessly. Perhaps you do not know that in this part of the world so doing in public is very bad form and a great offense to those present.

> No, in the Islamic Republic, the state and mosque are not one and the same. The Supreme Leader is a select spiritual being who oversees the work of the government to make sure that all we do is in compliance with the provisions of the Holy Quran. That is all. It is the laypeople who run the parliament, the ministries and all the rest of the organs of government. Can you not see that we, a layman and not a man of the cloth, are the President of the country?

> And as for your desire to learn from us, that is no problem either. We are a generous man. Although we do not operate a seminary or teach any formal classes, we will offer you tutorials from time to time. Of course, it all depends on what other pressing matters we may have to attend to.

THE FRAUD

> I guess I've been using up all the favors that I'm entitled to. I mean, about not using that explanation expression and invoking His Blessedness so often. Would you grant me another request, since you just repeated yourself by saying that you're a generous man?

THE FASCIST

> A conditional "yes."

THE FRAUD

> An earnest request. Please stop referring to your puny self as "we." It really makes you look even more absurd, if such a thing is possible. Who the hell are you, anyway? You said it yourself that the Seyyed can have your balls—if you even have any—if you don't jump every time he rattles your cage. So, you can't be all that important. What's wrong with being a bit self-effacing, like me?

THE FASCIST

> Glad you asked, "What's wrong?" If I had a face like yours, I would erase it completely, not just efface it. Being self-effacing somewhat covers the truly unworthy person you are. Yet, just to show you how agreeable I can be, I'll grant your request. Again, on the condition that I do not have pressing matters to attend to. See, I said "I," not "we," and I have employed the singular pronoun frequently before you submitted your request.

THE FRAUD

> Good. But, "pressing?"—that sounds ominous. Somehow it makes me shudder. You don't mean pressing the button you've been wanting to push, do you?

Hysterical laughter once again engulfs the Hitler incarnate. The Fraud nervously eyes the man, twitches uncontrollably, and starts picking his nose with his left pointer, as he usually does under stress. Psychologists say that these are symptoms of regression. When the person is stressed, he resorts to early childhood activities that he associates with safety and security. Under greater duress, he unconsciously attempts to go back to the illusory safety and security of the womb. And of course, he wouldn't fit. The shrinks keep pontificating that the ultimate womb for all life forms is Mother Earth. That's where the stressed run to—to the bosom of Mother Earth from where we all hail. You say this is absurd, a strange explanation? Well, what do you expect from that wacky lot, psychologists? They are just as rational and logical as theologians. And both these camps have been making a good living on the back of the world's gullible.

THE FRAUD

At the frenzied pace you're multiplying and operating those centrifuges to make enough enriched uranium bombs and missiles, and the way you become so giddy just mentioning "pressing," I'll never get a chance to set up my seminary, much less enjoy the amenities you promised.

Chuck it, man, that's my advice. You press the buttons, and then the Israelis will press theirs, then the Pakis get in the act, and the U.S., Russia and all the rest of the idiotic sons of bitches who have gotten the world into this nuclear-weapons mess will get into the act. And in no time we'll all make that metaphor of "ashes to ashes" a reality.

THE FASCIST

Relax, man, relax. I do not plan to unleash a mass annihilation. I intend to use it as leverage to keep the enemies of Islam at bay. If push comes to shove, I would use only a few tactical nuclear weapons and not the real heavy hitters.

THE FRAUD

That's so sweet. It's so kind of you. Is this your own thinking, or is it that of the Supreme Leader? Whose is it? Did he or you decide that, or did either one of you get that plan of action from On High?

THE FASCIST

It is all part of the plan of Allah Himself. Haven't you perused the holy passage, "He doeth what He willeth and ordaineth what He wisheth?"

THE FRAUD

So, tell me—why would a loving, caring creator who created both man and jinn, according to the Holy Quran, have such a plan for His very own creation and creatures? I can fully appreciate why He would rightfully want to rid His earth of creeps like you. But aren't there easier and more selective ways of doing that? Such as culling things, separating the sheep from the goats, so to speak?

THE FASCIST

You do not question Allah. He is not accountable to anyone, and all are accountable to Him. Once you assume your office of ayatollah, I suggest you seclude yourself at the shrine of Imam Hussein, your namesake, and pray for enlightenment. He shall assuredly relieve you of your bewilderment. I guarantee it.

THE FRAUD

Until such time, I suggest you keep occupying your itching fingers by picking your nose like you have been doing non-stop during the course of our meetings. It's a nauseating act and might, if you overdo it, perforate your nasal membrane. But the damage will be limited only to you and be well deserved.

THE FASCIST

Look who is calling the kettle black. I have noticed that you do the same. Do your fingers also itch? Or is it your unseemly nose that invites them to visit?

On that high note, they adjourned without shaking hands. Perhaps the nose-picking exchange made them both leery of going through the formality. I was noticing that, while initially they had been somewhat friendly and respectful of each other because they are "brothers in faith," their exchange was becoming increasingly hostile. This type of macho competition was not uncommon between Muslim rulers, and these two represented competing sects hostile to each other. Of course, the fact that the Fascist was basically blackmailing and coercing the Fraud with injury and death could not have helped the mood.

Act Fifteen

*T*he two combatants entered the arena for another round. It reminded me of a cockfight I had the misfortune of watching when I was a child. It was a horrible experience watching adult men act giddy with joy while urging their cock to bloody the other one before killing it completely. The scene was particularly disturbing to me because one of the two cocks was at least twice the size of the other. And here again, the difference in size of the two cocks revived that blood-curdling repressed memory. Yet, somehow I have a dreadful feeling that the puny and cocky cock is the one who will prevail.

THE FASCIST

> I just received a missive from the Leader. Something urgent needs me there. I have only a little time to finish our negotiations and no more. Ask what you like, carte blanche. Let me use the same phrase I used earlier: It is time to get down to brass tacks and not beat around the bush. Do you play or not?

THE FRAUD

> Did you actually get a missive that he needs you there, or is it just one of your arm-twisting methods to get what you want?

THE FASCIST

No, nothing like that. My plane is already being fueled and is prepared for takeoff. I have about two hours at the most, and we need to reach an agreement, at least on the overall plan. We will have plenty of time to iron out the details.

And let me say this: Do you want to be on the winning side or not? That is the main question you need to address—and address without delay. Recall what I said earlier! What we are offering you is indeed a win-win proposition. And we are not doing it out of the goodness of our heart—

THE FRAUD

See, you are wasting precious time. You don't need to assure me that anything you do or offer is coming from the goodness of your heart. I never ever suspected that, and you should remember what I said about jugs and what comes out of them is only what's in them—

THE FASCIST

I will ignore that snide remark. As I was saying before you rudely interrupted me, we do it because you are a perfect fit for the plan. Remember the word "plan" I mentioned the minute we met, when I heard your Arabic greeting? We knew all along that you are fluent in Arabic. And that is essential for the plan to work. If you could not speak Arabic, that would make the whole thing unpalatable even with a ton of honey. But, the way things turned out—undoubtedly due to His Blessedness working behind the scenes—you are the man. So, you will be the greatest fool in the world not to accept what is destined for you. I have a sense that you are simply playing hard to get, but you do want to answer the call of His

Blessedness. Let me explain, in a summary form since we do not have much time.

Islam is on the march. One out of four people on the planet is Muslim, and the demographics are rapidly changing in our favor. The biggest, if not the only, obstacle in the path of this march is the Great Satan. We need to subdue it, by hook or crook or both. And that is where you come in while you are still in a position of power to facilitate things.

The rest of the world is easy. Europe is a piece of cake. It is already in the oven baking and soon will be placed on the table. Just a couple of facts to buttress this self-evident statement that mentally challenged Harvard Law grads are not able to see for themselves.

We already have dozens of countries with Muslim constitutions or Muslim majorities. Much of Europe is teeming with Muslims whom the infidels imported over the past several decades to exploit as cheap labor while they did eat, drink and make merry. The chickens come to roost, so to speak. I mentioned demographics. The locals are not reproducing at replacement rates. Churches and synagogues have become caverns for mushroom growth instead of places for flocks of people. The *kuffar* do not produce children, and they do not even believe in their religions. They have no faith for their future, and that is why they do not produce children. Why bring children into the world that would cost them a fortune, stymie their self-indulging, hedonistic and materialistic life? They have figured it all out. No Harvard brain is needed for that. Are you with me?

THE FRAUD

Much as I hate it, yes, I'm still here.

THE FASCIST

Do not be rash. You will love it, and I will see the day that you would come and kiss my feet in gratitude for what I am offering you. And always keep the eight-by-eight Federal prison cell in the forefront of your mind. It helps dispel your illusions about yourself and the rosy future you are deluding yourself about.

As I was saying, just check the demographics for Europe. It is a domino effect of a sort. Spain and Italy are projected to cease in 20 years. What little reproduction is done there—I mean, children—is mostly contributed by the immigrants who are Muslims. The other nations such as Germany, France and whatnot are right there behind Spain and Italy.

So, that is Europe for you. I mean for *us*. Russia? The same story again. The vodka-saturated Russian's life expectancy, combined with all kinds of life-ending practices, are driving the Ruskies to extinction. The country has a huge Muslim population already. It will be a majority before your two little girls reach their twenties. Russia will become a Muslim state.

China, you may ask? Those trinket-making Chinese are reasonable people. We will see to it they get all the oil and gas they need to keep them happy making their trinkets. They will eventually come around too. They will have no choice with their one-child only policy and the aging population; they will be a huge geriatric ward incapable of even feeding themselves. Who is left? Japan? Forget it. I do not have time to go over the list country by country. What do you say?

THE FRAUD

> Hate to admit it, but you may be right.
> Although, of course, I wouldn't mind too much,
> since I definitely love the great religion of my
> youth.

THE FASCIST

> Of course, I am right. Have to keep our eyes on
> the big picture. It is a new order we are after—

THE FRAUD

> Is this the same "new order" that the Nazi
> psycho launched, and all it accomplished was
> to kill millions of people and transform much of
> Europe into a heap of rubble? He didn't get to
> finish the job, so *you* are trying to finish it?

THE FASCIST

> No, not at all, even though we admire that
> "Nazi psycho," as you call him. Our respective
> visions may have some elements in common,
> but that does not make them the same. The
> order I am talking about is the one that was
> launched by Rasul Allah himself.

THE FRAUD

> Almost 15 centuries ago—that is "new?"

THE FASCIST

> Well, it *is* new. You may want to call it a
> "renewal," you nitwit—have you not forgotten
> that I am in direct contact with the Sahib al-
> Zaman? His order will renew the world under
> the holy rule of Sharia. And you cannot build
> the new unless you get the old out of the way.
> The present systems, democratic, autocratic or
> whatnot, one and all are manmade—and look
> at what they have made of the world. One big
> Sodom, that is what it is. We, the devotees of
> the Imam Zaman Mahdi, have our assignment.

We are the demolition crew. Whether we like it or not, we have to use wrecking balls to do our job—

THE FRAUD

Just don't say, "Whether we like it or not." You *love* your job. Remember those bullets you fired in the heads of innocent prisoners? You yourself admitted how it thrilled you doing that. This time around you want bigger bullets to kill by the millions...

THE FASCIST

I recall when I was a little kid hearing a sermon in a mosque that made a deep impression on me. The mullah lectured on how important it is for people to get into an occupation they love, because—if they can earn a living at it—they are most likely to be good at it and will have fun doing it. Well, I really like what I do. I started as a low-level apprentice, and since I loved what I was doing, I did my job well— voila!—and here I am the foreman of the demolition team...

The despicable creature couldn't contain himself and roared with pleasure. For the first time, he also kept slapping his knee in the frenzy. How I wish that I could give him a hand in doing the slapping for him with all my force, not on his knee but on his truly nauseating face.

THE FRAUD

Hold on, wrecking ball. Get a hold of yourself. When I was a little kid, I also learned something that made a lasting impression on me. I learned that life is not a bowl of cherries. You don't always get everything you want and exactly the way you want it. Understand?

THE FASCIST

Go ahead, professor.

THE FRAUD

There is more than one way to skin a cat. Why don't we use a two-pronged approach? You keep your boys working 24/7 building the bomb, while I keep stalling for you by proposing sanctions that will never happen, because I won't seriously push for them, and the Ruskies and the Chinese would never come on board if the sanctions have any teeth at all. Why should they? Look at it from their standpoint: You're their cash cow, while being a huge pain for America. It keeps us—I mean, the U.S.—busy wasting time and resources trying to put out the fires you keep starting and fueling. That's how it is done. Although only because I'm under extreme duress from you, I'll do my end of the work. Are you with me?

Grinning from ear to ear, the Fascist nodded in response. On the contrary, I was chagrined to see this horrible scene unfolding itself in front of me: The leader of the Free World had all but capitulated to this diabolical plot for global domination. I could only think that he was doing so to save his own skin.

THE FRAUD

I'll also look the other way as money-worshipping Western firms keep selling you everything you need under the table, so to speak. Dubai is a gift of Allah Himself. It's a perfect transfer point for everything you need, right? I don't have to tell you this. You already know it and are making great use of it. And there are some boys in America who keep demanding I quarantine you. Or, at the very least do some serious arm-twisting to stop the flow of refined oil to your country.

It's really insane. You cats are floating on oil, and yet you don't have the facilities and expertise to refine enough of the stuff for yourselves, so you have to import the refined crap.

THE FASCIST

Speaking of oil, America is incurably addicted to it—although you are doing your best to give the United States an alternative energy plan, specifically to keep your money out of our terrorist hands. That is something which must not happen, of course, because Iran has the world's third largest reserves—envious? Yes, we know you are after our oil. After all, even if you are an internationalist, you do not want your chosen homeland to fall apart, do you? We have the oil—now you are going to have to beg to get at it. Oh, especially since that national disaster in the Mexican Gulf—how will you recover from that without our help? We had a feeling that if that really happened, your country would start to go down—

THE FRAUD

Wait just a minute—"if that really happened?!" What are you talking about? Did you just confess to sabotaging the oil rig in the Gulf? Talking heads say that it could cost us the country. You're saying you're behind it? I should strangle you with my own hands.

THE FASCIST

Well, your American Jews at Goldman Sachs *were* very useful—they did promise much of their gains for shorting the Gulf of Mexico rig on the stock market the day before the disaster. But do not lump us in with those Zionist criminals just yet, as we are not admitting our guilt or complicity in anything.

And, I must say that those are no longer *your* hands. They belong to us.

THE FRAUD

I see—you really have me over a barrel, so to speak. So, then, you carry on with the project, and I do my part to make sure that no serious problem comes your way. I'll do that for as long as I am in office. You got me really worried about 2012. I think that you might be right. Many Americans are fed-up with me. My constituency, the left that worked very hard to get me in office, is thoroughly disappointed for me not implementing their agenda exactly as they want it. The idiots seem to think that I can rule by fiat, like you boys do. And the right always hated my guts anyway. And the middle is dangerously gravitating to the right—my ship is in turbulent waters and likely to sink.

What's the matter? Cat got your tongue? You're letting me talk without constantly interrupting me. Or is it medication time, and that's why you're yawning non-stop and fidgeting?

THE FASCIST

Your ship is not "likely" to sink; it is *guaranteed* to sink. Mark my word. So you have got to move your arse and not waste time covering it. You will have to stop being the vacillating, spineless idiot that you have been. Sure enough it got you the Presidency, but now is crunch time, and people are after your tail fast and hard. You have to do what we want you to do and be all ready to bail out. Yes, your ship has already sprung a bunch of leaks. It might not even last until 2012. You do not have a minute to waste—

THE FRAUD

> If I don't have a minute to waste, what am I doing spending hours with a creature like you?

THE FASCIST

> Let us have a short recess. I really need to settle my nerves. Then I will try my hardest to be nice to you

Before the Fraud could speak, the little worm snapped his fingers, and his genie appeared in the person of the Thick Thug with the tray full of medication. Through long experience, the Thick Thug had come to anticipate his master's medication need and had learned that any delays in having the stuff ready could unleash the deadly wrath of the little tyrant.

Act Sixteen

*A*ll medicated and refreshed, the meeting of the two dope-saturated clowns resumed. The Fascist seemed woozy from the lingering effect of his medication, while the Fraud appeared to be energized and eager to proceed.

THE FRAUD

> We must work the system from inside and make it implode, and not have the need for you to explode it. As you pointed out, democracy is a flawed and dysfunctional man-made system of governance. It doesn't stand a chance against the will of Allah and His design for the rule of the Ummah. The brotherhood can take over from within. You're looking at living proof—

THE FASCIST

> Living? You could have fooled me...

This sophomoric remark was followed by an uproarious "ha, ha, ha!" I snickered at all the stupid and juvenile jokes: As the man said, comedians they are not.

THE FRAUD

> Okay, wise guy. Would you shut up and let me finish? I know that we don't love each other, don't even like each other. But we both love Islam, so that we just need to put up with each other for the sake of a much greater purpose.

THE FASCIST

> Love you? That is an impossibility. Remember, we do not have homosexuals in Iran. Like you? Not a chance. Despise you? Absolutely.

THE FRAUD

> Still in denial? I'll just have to ignore you, you little insect, and go on. As I was saying, democracy is so flawed that it can be imploded from within—what did the Muslim Brotherhood say? To wit: "We will sabotage the West's miserable house from within." Again, here I am, born to a Kenyan from a Muslim family, and, without even having to show the American people my records, I have worked the democratic system to become President of the United States of America, still the greatest nation in the world—even if you or I hate it— but *I'm* the one who became President of this powerful country, not you.

> Anyway, Europe is teeming with Muslims. Canada can't admit the Ummah fast enough, nor can the U.S. Before you know it, Muslims will become an insurmountable force. They—or "we," if you prefer—can win elections all across these infidel lands. Keep in mind what politicians are like. You are one of them, so *you* ought to know. Politicians are like lawyers and all other mercenary types. They are for sale. And we can buy them by the hundreds, not only with money but also with votes. Get it, Mr. Dense?

THE FASCIST

> Yes, I dig, Mr. Soft. Go on.

THE FRAUD

> Islam enjoys a large and influential ally among the non-Muslims. Lenin called them "useful

idiots." He, Lenin, said that these people lived in liberal democracies but unwittingly furthered the work of communism. Well, today's world is also full of them. I hate calling them "useful *idiots*" since they *are* useful to us. But for now I'll call them that to share with you their psychological profile provided to me by expert psychologists upon my request—

THE FASCIST

Since you have the services of these expert psychologists, you should have taken advantage of them and asked them to provide your *own* psychological profile. The very profile of a useless idiot!

I'll just call a "laugh" the hideous howl that followed the Fascist's put-down of the Fraud, and leave it at that.

THE FRAUD

As I was saying, hear me out since the definition of "useful idiot" is most likely going to fit *you.*

Useful idiots are naïve; they are foolish, they are ignorant of facts. They are unrealistically idealistic dreamers either willfully in denial or deceptive. They hail from the ranks of the chronically unhappy; they are anarchists and aspiring revolutionaries; they are neurotics who are at war with life, the disaffected alienated from government, corporations and just about any and all institutions of society. The useful idiot can be a billionaire, a movie star, a renowned scholar, a politician, or from any other segment of the population. Arguably, the most useful variant of the Useful Idiot is the "Politically Correct." He is the master practitioner of euphemism, hedging, doubletalk and outright deception.... Are you listening?

THE FASCIST

> I know the kind very well, as my regime is full
> of these rubes and pigeons, and we use them
> all over the world. But saying that *I* am one is
> pure, unadulterated crap! I will not stand—

THE FRAUD

> The report goes on. It's too lengthy to share it
> all with you here. I'll send you a hard copy of it
> so you can better develop self-understanding.
> Just one more point from the report: It said
> that the most dangerous of useful idiots is the
> religious fanatic, kind of saying the obvious.
> They said those are the people who don
> explosive belts and detonate themselves in any
> gathering, as directed by their handlers. I bet
> you would do that if the honorable Seyyed,
> *your* handler, told you to. I'd guess you either
> would have to do that or eat the delicacy kebab
> that the Supreme Leader would provide for you,
> as you mentioned before.

*This time the Fraud laughed himself silly. The fascist
creep maintained his silence while sporting an
expression that was a picture worth a thousand words:
the kind of expression that a sudden skunk spray
elicits. Although I could see no literal skunk, I clearly
could witness the presence of two virtual ones. The
lanky "American" waited for a minute to enjoy the
tortuous face of his repugnant company, then the
conversation continued.*

THE FASCIST

> Leave my kebab out of this. But, you are
> correct: We *can* exploit these useful idiots to
> the maximum. Again, we are the wrecking
> balls, and these idiots are our inadvertent crew.
> We simply connect with them and entice them
> to keep on attacking the system wherever they
> live. We promise them the skies and whatever

they may want. We even put things in writing if
they ask for it. Once it is done, we clean them
up, get rid of them for good—that is how it is
always done. The useful idiots stand up for *our*
rights, and then once we are in the majority, we
either subjugate them as *dhimmis* or kill them
off. No biggie to us, as they are but dirty
infidels. So, we might call these useful idiots
"dhimwits." They are like termites. They can eat
up the fabric of any system from within...

And all along some have considered *you* to be a
card-carrying member of the Useful Idiots
Club, as you defined them. And I fully agree
with them in part: You yourself are indeed an
idiot, but also useful to the cause.

THE FRAUD

I'll ignore the idiot part and accept the useful
attribution. To my thinking, playing games is
over. I try not to insult you and level with you. I
wish you would do the same.

So in the end, you're blackmailing me. But
what about your *own* crimes, which are many
and legendary?

THE FASCIST

Ah, but I admittedly do bad things, and
everybody knows it. But they don't care! In fact,
I think they admire my badness. Did you not
see the photograph of me signing the deal of
selling enriched uranium to Turkey? All the
while the meeting was held in Brazil—now,
Turkey and Brazil are *America's* allies, not
ours—so how did we do that? And the Western
fools will be letting Turkey into the EU soon,
very soon! Who has won now?

THE FRAUD

Sigh. That's the main reason I'm capitulating to you now—the West has already lost. Here you are, one of the world's major supporters of terrorism, and you get this royal treatment from allies of the *victims* of this terrorism!

Western intel has told us for years that the Islamic Republic of Iran is the paymaster of many of the atrocities and acts of terrorism. We know, for instance, that the Pakis in England were the ones who got caught for their horrendous plan of blowing up several planes full of innocent civilians in midair. Again, the West's spook agencies say that your boys have developed the "Islamic Cocktail" for the Pakis to use—a "cocktail" served free of charge to transport the passenger to a different destination, the good Muslim servers to Allah's Paradise and the infidel passengers to the devil's hell.

As you may be able to tell, I'm conflicted because of many issues with which I disagree with your regime, which is evil, frankly. You're basically trying to turn me from Anakin to Darth Vader, in order to betray Western civilization, Emperor Palpatine. To make myself feel better about this pending serious compromise of my integrity, let me confess: I'm intrigued by the spiritual part of your deal, even though it's a heresy from the Sunni perspective. But, I guess I can give it a go. How's this:

I'm with you. Shi'a Islam is the true Islam, and our goal is to do everything we can to make it the one-and-only religion of the world. But this is a tall order. Short of the Imam Zaman Mahdi appearing and doing it himself, we have to have a multiple strategy. I for one don't want to bank on your quick and dirty solution. I mean, setting off a chain reaction of nuclear conflagration to give the Imam the boost he needs out of the well, so he can take it from there—

THE FASCIST

Thank you for that wonderful display of sycophancy—I hardly think I can trust you, and I find your lack of faith disturbing. Moreover you are still an irreverent piece of trash, the way you think and speak about the holy Imam. It is too bad that we need you and have to work with you. Otherwise, it would give me a great pleasure to cut off your tongue right this minute. No more mocking the Imam, you hear?

THE FRAUD

You can't take a joke? Come on—I told you I'm with you. It's just that your Middle Eastern flowery and flattery way of speech is not something I was raised with. I see that it upsets you. I'll stop. I promise. Let me go on.

At this point, I could no longer tell what the American president's motivation was, but I figured that either all the tyrant's threats, along with the drugging—another typical brainwashing tactic—had broken the younger and less conniving man's reserve. Either that or he was just scamming the conniver to get out of that dangerous place.

THE FASCIST

Keeping your word would be a novel experience for you. Let us see if you can do it. Go ahead, tell me about the multiple strategies you have in mind.

THE FRAUD

> I'll do my level best to give you all the time I
> can possibly give you while I am in office. I
> mean, I'll keep threatening sanctions, even use
> of force only to buy you time. That's a promise,
> to keep you happy making your favorite toys. In
> the meantime, we need to enlist as many
> people as we can to our cause—and there are
> legions of them who can help us without really
> knowing it. Are you with me?

THE FASCIST

> Unfortunately, yes, although I would rather be
> with the devil himself...

*The Fascist couldn't resist getting back at his guest,
after he had made a similar comment in response to the
latter asking the same question. No need to tell you that
he again went into his convulsive laughter. What I do
need to tell you is how badly I wished he never had
never come out of the convulsion but had headed
instead into Mother Earth. Although I fear Mother Earth
would rightly refuse to accept him.*

THE FRAUD

> You finished? Perhaps you are right. You can't
> bank on my promises. But what *I* can bank on
> with complete certainty is your stupid
> impertinency and sense of humor. I'm serious.
> Stop being frivolous, and let's get things done.

THE FASCIST

> Give you my word. My Scout's honor, although
> I have never been a Scout.

THE FRAUD

> They wouldn't take you. By the time you got to
> be Scout's age, you had a yard-long rap sheet.
> It's all in *your* file. Now, as I was saying, let me
> go on. While you are busy making the bombs,

and I am looking the other way, we need to prepare things on the ground. For one, democracy is not our enemy. It's our best ally. I'll explain that later, if we have time. Then, there is a legion of useful idiots spread all over the world who can be most effectively exploited. To do that, to take advantage of what democratic nations provide us, and to enlist the useful idiots fully on our side, we need to moderate our rhetoric and change some of our tactics...

THE FASCIST

I know you taught law at the University of Chicago. Chuck your professorial verbiage and get to the point.

THE FRAUD

Okay, obscene, rude little man, I'll do the best I can.

THE FASCIST

It is not the size of the dog in the fight but the size of fight in the dog that counts. Go ahead— do your best, big dog.

His last remark was shocking because Muslims consider dogs to be najis *or "unclean," and the worst name they can call someone is a "dog." But here the creep implied that* he himself *was a little dog with a big bite. Perhaps he couldn't resist flaunting his knowledge of the English idioms and expressions that he had been using, appropriately or not, all along. Who knows what goes on in the cesspool sitting on his puny neck?*

THE FRAUD

You're little, all right. But try, if you can, to zip your huge mouth and let me go on. Do you and your people pull the strings on some of the things that in my opinion hurt the cause of the Ummah? I know you finance and arm the

Shi'ite Hezbollah in Lebanon as well as the Sunni Hamas to keep on harassing Israel— again, you're one of the world's major sponsors of terrorism. And that's a dubious strategy in any case, but you have your reasons, so I'll just have to go along with that. What about suicide bombings and assassinations? They backfire, you know.

THE FASCIST

That kind of work is stupid. We are in the big game. We do not go after individuals and not even handfuls. Operating like that is like trying to swat mosquitoes one at a time. You have got to drain the swamp to get rid of them, right? We have bigger fish to fry—

THE FRAUD

Don't say that word. Coming from you it's not frying fish but mass-frying *people* that you have in mind. I want to get up and choke you myself, so you won't get a chance to fry anything. Yet, killing you, as you aptly put it, is only swatting one very dangerous mosquito, and thousands of others of the most dangerous kind of useful idiots—the religious fanatics— will be just too happy to replace you!

THE FASCIST

Calm down. Let me finish. Look, we did not even carry out the fatwa of the beloved Imam Khomeini on Salman Rushdie, did we? That filth is still alive and has become a celebrity in the *kafir* world. No, we do not even have our people retaliate against the murdering Sunnis in Iraq and Pakistan who bomb our funeral processions and even our mosques. You do not have to teach us any lessons on this subject, professor. We are way ahead of you. So, say something useful.

THE FRAUD

> Okay, fine. I'll try. The wind is at our back. It really is. The people in the West are in a frenzy. They are tripping over each other, as well as tripping each other, in their relentless pursuit of money. They try to make as much money as they can by any means they can to get whatever money can get for them, which is just about everything that means anything to them. They literally eat, drink and make merry, for they indeed know that there is no tomorrow for them. Tomorrow is Allah's...

> We don't have the time for me to give you the whole body of evidence and in great detail. I'll just give a synopsis of it. Do you understand what "synopsis" is?

THE FASCIST

> Yes, something that windbags like you are incapable of. So, my advice, do not promise something you cannot deliver.

THE FRAUD

> Okay, Mr. Congeniality. Is it medication time? I've noticed that you're able to function in a semblance of civility for only a couple of hours, and then you start fraying at the edges. Only after you take your medication, do you become somewhat tolerable in human company. You want a short recess? Just say so.

THE FASCIST

> A short recess.

Act Seventeen

*T*he short recess lasted an hour and forty-five minutes. While the Fascist smoked his medicine at a leisurely pace, the Fraud went along for a free ride by deeply inhaling the air-filled smoke. As I sat watching the scene on tape, I bit my nails waiting for them to resume their deliberation. I noticed their personalities changed when they were high from inhaling, likely explaining the strange switching back and forth between moods I was witnessing.

THE FRAUD

May I continue where we left off?

THE FASCIST

You may, but try the synopsis bit and stop being verbose. I am beginning to feel a certain kinship, this time with the biblical character of Job, putting up with your diatribes. Make it short. Okay?

THE FRAUD

Okay, sweetness. You're as sweet as your medicine. You've eaten it enough times to know how sweet it is. Maybe that's where you get your sweetness from, or most likely what you are is a genetic aberration.

THE FASCIST

I said, make it short.

THE FRAUD

Okay. As I was saying, the wind is at our back. Although it won't be smooth sailing, we shall sail to the shore of destiny—

THE FASCIST

Sh—, man. Do not wax poetic for me, Shakespeare incarnate. What happened to your synopsis? Cut to the chase.

THE FRAUD

Islam is making tremendous headway in the Dar al-Harb, the "house of war," the *kuffar* lands. Muslim apologists are in a race with one another to see who wins the prize for singing the praises of the holy Islamic faith. And there are some literal prizes involved. Saudis are particularly into this business—they helped me with my college expenses, but that was small fry. They have set up Islamic studies programs in a number of top notch Western universities with endowed chairs. Occupiers of these chairs, the professors, have a sweetheart deal: They keep singing all the way to the bank with pockets full of Saudi money. These universities are so corrupt with the filthy lucre that they have accepted sharia banking and finance, which requires the funding of Islamic "charities" and will bring much money to the Ummah—and the terrorists.

THE FASCIST

Okay, you can stop singing the praises of your *former* paymasters, since you will be working for us soon. Speaking of Sharia-compliant finance, if you are wise you will coerce the Zionist bankers to make sure some of those *zakat* payments go to our ayatollahs, so you can get yourself a large piece of the pie.

Anyway, tell me, are your handlers still ponying up? That is why you are singing their praises in my presence?

THE FRAUD

No, you little pony, or is it little *phony*? They are not ponying up, as you like to put it. Not to me. I'm beyond the pocket-change stage. Anyway, let me go on. The public has come to venerate these academics. Even if they fart, the duped masses take it as a new aroma to be cherished. See what I mean? These paid mouthpieces are worth every penny the Saudis you despise pay them. The return on investment is by far better than the money you dole to Hezbollah and Hamas.

THE FASCIST

Okay, Mr. Economist *par expellant*. Last time, you won the Nobel *Piss* Prize for your illustrious non-doing in promoting peace. Next year, they ought to give you the prize again for your acumen in economics and investment policy. What kind of returns are Americans getting from playing gendarme of the world, which costs "your" country billions of dollars? Save it, will you? Give me the synopsis and only on the topic at hand.

THE FRAUD

Right. What I am saying is that it has become most fashionable to sing the praises of Islam, attributing any and all mayhem and violence committed by our devoted brethren not to Islam but to a small "fringe" of hoodlums who happen to be nominally Muslim. Anyone who dares to sound the alarm about what we are doing and in any way says anything negative about Islam is immediately labeled "hatemonger," "racist" and "Islamophobe," etc., and is made an outcast—assuming that some of our brothers don't take him out first, like what they did to the Dutch filmmaker Theo van Gogh. And your earlier lie notwithstanding about not being in the business of ridding one mosquito at a time, you and your people—who included paid Afghan assassins—had a whole slew of men and women murdered both in Iran and abroad. You have the list, so I'll limit myself to the synopsis, as you keep reminding me, and won't recite their names for you—

The Thick Thug barged into the room without knocking and announced that the plane was ready to take off and that his Excellency had only 15 minutes to conclude his meeting.

The Fascist motioned him out with a royal sweep of his hand and turned to the Fraud.

THE FASCIST

I believe we had a good meeting. We did not have enough time to cover everything in as great detail as we wanted to. But, we got to know each other very well, and we agreed that, although we severely dislike each other, we still must work together for the greater cause.

You failed to give me the synopsis of the last point you were making. No matter. I'll summarize our agreement, and all *you* have to say is to agree completely or turn it down altogether. No time or room for horse trading. Understand?

THE FRAUD

So, say I join you, *if* you're even in office—the chance of you being thrown out is very good.

THE FASCIST

> Perhaps, but not if you help us, enlisting the Great Satan to "meddle" in our affairs in a constructive way.

THE FRAUD

> The synopsis, please. The plane is about to take off. Maybe, just maybe, one of our trigger-happy jet jockeys will swish a missile through your tailpipe—I mean, the *plane's* tailpipe—and sully the Afghan airspace with bits of your stinking body and that of your Thick Thug attendant. Hurry up and finish.

THE FASCIST

> That is a wish you will never live long enough to see realized, while *I* can see *you* chain-smoking in an eight-by-eight Federal prison as clearly as I see you right now picking your nose.

> To avoid that certain bleak future and to win both in this world and the next, you have no choice but to accept our offer. You do what I have asked you, and we guarantee you a life of great comfort with all the amenities that any man can desire. You have my word on that.

> Here is our agreement—I will summarize it for you:

> • You pull—gradually and in close consultation with us, all hush-hush and private of course—America's killers out of Iraq, Afghanistan and the other former Soviet states the U.S. has bribed. We will be your contractor for the job of eliminating Al-Qaeda and the Taliban, which we hate even more than you do anyway, because they are nothing but infidel CIA and Mossad fronts—in another words, just an American and

Zionist plot to defame the holy faith of Islam. Earlier, I did sketch the bare outline of how we do this one.

- You get the Zionist dogs, the Neocons and Christian fundamentalist retards off our backs—or, at the very least, sabotage their plans so that we can do our work with minimal harassment.

- Use *taqiyya* and *kitman* to full advantage, whenever and wherever you can, finding comfort and confidence that you are only obeying the instruments Allah has given us to faithfully carry out his agenda. Keep on praising Islam, even more than what you have been doing. In any way you can, perhaps in subtle ways, praise the true Shi'a faith, especially Twelver Shi'ism. Perhaps try to pass that as part of your philosophy of fair play and even-handedness in dealing with the Muslim world—you cannot just favor the Sunni majority. In so doing, soften the masses for their full conversion in the future.

- Keep on talking the big talk with your big mouth about pressuring us, imposing crippling sanctions and even quarantining us. You know and we know that our two well-paid Security Council members, Russia and China, will not go along with any of it, and you would be issuing threats as worthless as America's treasury bonds.

- Do nothing to pressure banks and companies to stop doing business with us. On the contrary, see what you can do, using your huge conniving talent, to help us get some of the parts we need for our aging airplanes and the new weapons. Also, supply us with some conventional weapons—

we will give you the list—through intermediaries so that we can arm our Afghani brothers to pretend to smoke that bogus bin Laden and his gang out of their caves and into their graves, if they were even alive or in caves to begin with. Otherwise, we would smoke the Sheik out, something the big-mouth Texan bragged about but failed to achieve—probably because the Arab phony is a CIA and Mossad asset in the first place. But, we need the weapons, so I will tell you whatever you or your current backers want to hear.

- Realistically speaking, it is going to take us another two years before we will have what we are after—the bombs, along with the missiles to carry them far and wide and land them with pin-point accuracy. Here, we have a major need for your state-of-the-art supercomputers—only a few of them. Somehow you have got to figure out how to help us. If you cannot supply them, look the other way, as the Germans are more than happy to oblige us with anything we want, no questions asked.

- We also need foodstuffs: Wheat, rice, cheese, legumes and a whole lot more. American farmers grow them like weeds. My people will give you the list. It is a long one. See to it we get them. You make us happy, and you make happy the thousands of farmers like the ones in Iowa who launched you toward the Presidency. You can do that openly by claiming it is part of your soft diplomacy policy, which aims to coax us around, as well as demonstrating goodwill toward Muslim nations.

- Above all else, we need to buy time. And you are the Allah-sent best time-seller. As I just said, we need at least two years, and you are the best person to see to it that we get the time we need. What you can do is to keep issuing one "last chance" ultimatum every couple of months or so. The Texan used that trick *ad nauseam*. For your part, be more creative than that moron. Change things. Say that you are getting signals from Tehran that they—that is, *we*—are willing to accept your terms with slight modifications. And we see to it that we also raise our hot-air balloons to keep the public looking *up*, instead of looking *at* what we keep on doing. Send high-level emissaries to meet our high-level people in Geneva. Crap like that. You are a master of deception. Use your talent and buy us time.

What do *you* get out of the deal? I may have to repeat myself, but I hope you bear with me. After all, this is summarizing. In addition to having a guaranteed top of the line life in the Islamic Republic instead of the Federal prison, you have my word that our pursuit of the bomb is only precautionary—a sort of insurance, so to speak. We will patiently wait to see if the imploding from within happens in the *kafir* land with America, our archenemy, ending up flat dead on its fat belly. We will resort to explosion only if the implosion fizzles. We will reserve the bomb as the very last arrow in our quiver.

Apparently thinking he had pretty much sealed the deal, the Fascist grinned broadly at the Fraud before concluding.

The Fascist

I have got to run. No time for questions, much less for equivocation. If any ambiguity remains, we will iron it out later. Do you or do you not, Hussein, want to sign on, or are you still not sure? Yes or no. Which is it?

Oh, and by the way, just in case the threat of arrest is not sufficient motivation, we have already arranged for those paid Afghani assassins to look after your family if you decide you do not want to become a Shi'a ayatollah. And please do not forget that you yourself are publicly an apostate—there are already those in the Ummah who want to kill you. I do not believe you are an apostate, but you are definitely a heretic while you remain under Sunni influence, and a heretic is as good as an apostate—both need to be killed. You may not even find safety in the prison cell you are headed for if your Kenyan birth is proved. We already believe the Birthers anyway, since you clearly *are* a Manchurian Candidate—luckily for us.

Also, do not forget that by becoming a Shi'a, you will no longer be under Zionist control. In addition, with our oil reserves, you can become very wealthy indeed—as long as we are kept in power. In fact, if you do not play ball with us, as you say, you will not see one drop of our oil—ever. If you want to save America, as I earlier promised that you could, this is the only way. Look at it this way, you will be a great hero for saving the United States! Just stick with us. If you do not, we will help to bring off Armageddon anyway, to hasten the return of our beloved Twelfth Imam.

I was sitting on the edge of my seat, waiting for the response to this culminating conversation. The Fraud first turned green at the violent threats, which he apparently took quite seriously. Next, head in hands he appeared for several minutes to be considering all the options, including the promise of increased wealth and at least a decent position of power. Finally, he gazed up at heaven, slapped his knee, leapt to his feet and approached the Fascist, while fairly shouting his response.

THE FRAUD

Well, well, well. You really have me over a barrel, don't you? So, I might as well submit and embrace the righteous cause of the pure and holy Sahib al-Zaman, and I do enlist myself as his unwavering devoted foot-soldier. I agree with everything you summarized. May Allah, the merciful, the compassionate, bless and assist us in our undertaking. May He, by our work, cleanse His earth from the accursed Satan and His creatures. Praise Allah!

In return, the Fascist brayed his reply at the top of his voice, in celebration of a hard-fought victory.

THE FASCIST

O Sahib al-Zaman, O Lord of the Age, O Mahdi, we plead with you to expedite your return and rise up out of the Jamkaran well. We give you our honor pledge to do whatever you inspire and command us to do to hasten your coming and assuming your-much-prayed-for reign.

Then the two Dr. Strangelove mutations loudly praised Allah in unison.

THE FASCIST AND THE FRAUD

Allahu Akbar, Allahu Akbar, Allahu Akbar!

About the Author

Amil Imani is an Iranian-American writer, poet, novelist, essayist, literary translator, public speaker and political analyst who has been writing and speaking out about the danger of radical Islam both in America and internationally. He has become a formidable voice for the struggling people of his native land of Iran. Born in Tehran, Imani moved to the United States during the Islamic Revolution of 1979.

Imani has both promoted American patriotism, and encouraged democracy for Iran. He has been published in numerous newspapers and magazines around the world as well as in thousands of internet magazines, websites and blogs. Amil's writings can be found on his website, www.AmilImani.com. Imani is also one of the founders of Former Muslims United, which came to existence in September 2009.

LaVergne, TN USA
06 August 2010
192356LV00001B/4/P